Dedicated to Alex McClelland aka Pow

CONTENTS

Part Three: What Next?

Part Four: Resources

CONTRIBUTORS

Jeremy Banks (Banx) is an award-winning cartoonist who has illustrated books and periodicals including *Private Eye*, the *Financial Times*, www.thereaper.rip and many more. He is husband to Eleanor and father to four kids. @BanxCartoons.

Sarah Jane Baker writes about LGBTQ+ issues. She's a poet, violinist, bricklayer, welder and a published author from Camberwell, South London. She's the world's longest serving transgender prisoner, currently in her 30th year of incarceration in HMP Lewes (a male institute). @LiferSarah on Twitter.

Darcey Hartley talks about her experiences of growing up with Ian (her dad) serving an indefinite sentence. She's 16, from Lancashire and is currently doing her GCSEs. She hopes to become a probation officer. Ian is currently in HMP Humber. @DarceyHartley on Twitter.

Jon Gulliver was born and raised in London. He's a son, a big sports fan, and an Arsenal supporter. He has been locked up since the age of 14. Jon has served in many infamous jails including Feltham. He is currently still in the system and is now on the right track with a bit of luck.

Julia Howard writes about female prisons. She's from Manchester and is mother to two daughters, Kiah and Macy. She's the North West Regional Manager at User

Voice and a trustee of the Prison Radio Association. She is a former student of Manchester Metropolitan University and ex–prisoner of HMP Styal. @JuHoward77 on Instagram.

Elliot Murawski talks about drug recovery, funerals and temporary release. He's currently serving in an open prison as he writes this but will be released by the time this book hits the shelves. He's been addicted to heroin and other hard drugs since his teens, but will have been clean for over two years by the time he gets out.

Lisa Selby talks about being a 'prison wife'. She's an artist, educator, activist and partner of Elliot. She's originally from Essex but now teaches in Nottingham. Lisa and Elliot work together on the highly recommended @BlueBagLife Instagram account.

You can find Carl Cattermole on social media on @HMPSurvival.

INTRODUCTION

Newspapers say prison is a holiday camp, movies say it's a bloodbath and the government says it's a place of rehabilitation and education. Confused? When I was preparing to go to prison I definitely was, so I sat on a park bench with my mate Andrew (who served two years for painting graffiti) and asked him about the reality. Then when I hit prison my first cellmate Jeroen (a street homeless guy locked up for shoplifting bacon) told me the rest. The information in this book is conveyed to you in the vein of their advice to me.

Over months and years prisoners and their families become experts in coping with the system. We find out about the obscure charities that specialise in exactly what we need, we find small bits of financial support the government keeps well hidden, we find out about the rights we have when it comes to internal prison adjudications, we find the things that preserve our dignity and our personalities from the slide of institutionalisation. But once it's all over, we just leave all that information behind.

This book tries to compile all of that knowledge. I wrote the original version with an electronic monitoring tag around my ankle, fresh out of jail, confused and angry but wanting to turn everything I'd seen into something proactive and positive. The idea was basic – a 'survival guide'. Text only, black and white. My mate who was a nightshift cleaner at a Canary Wharf bank illegally photocopied it 1,000 times. I picked the stacks of paper up at 4am with a camping bag, got my mates to help paginate and staple it together, then distributed it for free. It was evident that a lot of people needed this information and that a lot of people who might never face jail want the nuanced and up-to-date truth about British prisons written by an ex-prisoner – not a script writer, journalist or policy advisor who has never even been arrested.

This new edition is written with the same intent and same energy but it's so much more complete than the original – expert contributors have given a window into the experience of female prisoners, child prisoners, LGBTQ+ prisoners, and the partners and children of prisoners who serve a sentence of their own in the community. At the back of this book you'll find contact details for the organisations I mention throughout.

Prison writing has often been 'one bloke's struggle against the system' and I'm not knocking any of that because some of it is phenomenal, but this is a very different book – it's simply a factual, up-to-date and practical guide which reflects what prison really is: a mix of technical legal systematic bullshit mixed with emotions that are really hard to understand. It's not lighthearted because the prison system isn't – and if you find it hard to read, then remember that over 80,000 people are currently living this 24/7.

I guarantee that we will offend the usual media suspects: the banter, jokes and ways of swerving the system will most likely lead those people to say I'm encouraging bad behaviour, but the reality is I'm writing this in good faith. If we're honest about the justice system, we could actually make it work for society. More transparency, more trust, less crime, fewer victims.

If you read this book as a prisoner, a prison officer, healthcare worker, victim of crime, a governor or you just have something to say, then email me. I will blog it at prisonism. co.uk and it may be included in future editions. And, if you're part of the wider public and you are shocked by the gritty realities, then don't get too sad – I conclude the book with really amazing ways you can be proactive and get involved.

PART ONE: THE BASICS

FIRST THINGS FIRST

Leave all your out-of-date prison stereotypes at the door. Prison these days is completely different to what you might expect – in their populations, their operation and their entire purpose. The prison population is very skewed towards the disadvantaged side of Britain, but inside you'll meet everyone from privately-educated fraudsters to dangerous drivers, knife crime kids, weed dealers, squatters (it's a crime to live in an empty house), and a huge number of drug addicts and mentally ill people.

Eighty thousand people from different backgrounds are coping in 80,000 different ways in 150 institutions governed by national rules, local rules and often multiple contradictory rules for the same thing: the kind of rules you've seen broken a million times suddenly get dropped on you if a staff member woke up on the wrong side of bed. For an institution whose middle name is rules, you'll be amazed. The inconsistencies are so extreme that I've invented an acronym – C.R.A.P., or Confusing Rules Applied Patchily (the prison service, like most public authorities, love cranky acronyms, so this is a tribute). This book will serve as a broad guide but refer to *Inside Time* (the national prison newspaper) and relevant charities for more detailed info about specific places and scenarios.

Everything illegal in this book is very well known to the authorities: every 'screw' (prison officer) knows that prisoners have 'techs' (illegal phones), they know we charge them with games consoles and stash them round the toilet U-bend, they know you can use toothpaste to build secret cupboard compartments and they know how we make jail velcro. The very few things they don't know shouldn't see the light of day in this book, on social media or anywhere else.

The third thing is that you are not a lemming – if I discuss something illegal then it's up to you what you do. You should always seek expert legal advice.

AFTER ARREST

Let's start right at the beginning. When you're arrested, going 'no comment' (not saying a word) to the police is so important that I can't fail to mention it here, until you have legal representation with you – I might have avoided the whole justice system if someone had explained this to me as a kid. Always be honest and logical with honest and logical people, never be either with a system that is neither.

If you've been arrested you'll be released on bail or you'll be remanded. **Bail** is release from the police station while under investigation. If you're charged with a crime then you'll be on 'post-charge bail' and given a court date. If you're not charged then you'll be on 'pre-charge bail', which is now limited to 28 days but can be extended to three months by a senior police officer or longer by a magistrate. There might be conditions (mine included a curfew, reporting to a police station every single day and not being allowed to contact my best friends). Breaking these conditions isn't a separate crime but you can be arrested and the police might try to fight for you to be sent to prison without yet being convicted.

You haven't been convicted of a crime yet but bail is a period of extreme uncertainty and is a mental sentence of its own: sleepless nights worrying about potential prison time, what people will think – night and daymares about employment, housing, family and money. Bear in mind you haven't been found guilty of a crime yet. If you still think Britain operates by 'innocent until proven guilty' then that's another old idea you need to leave at the door.

Remand is when you're sent to jail before you've been sentenced. It's understandable for seriously dangerous criminals but you'd be surprised – around 10 per cent of people in prison right now are on 'remand' and 10 per cent of those will be completely acquitted and a further 14 per cent given a non-custodial sentence. This means that at any one time around 2,000 prisoners shouldn't even be in prison.

Remand prisoners get slightly more privileges in the system – more visits, your own clothes and slightly more spending ability (if you've got money being sent in). However, you get no compensation or financial assistance whatsoever upon release, regardless of the damage that's been done to you and your life. They don't even give you the £46 release grant, or cover the cost of a ticket home (if you've still get one).

If you're on remand for a less serious crime you have the right to talk to a Bail Information Officer but it's often more difficult than it sounds. I'd recommend talking to PAS (Prisoners' Advice Service): these lot deserve a little introduction: they provide advice and also run support clinics inside many prisons.

Court deserves its own survival guide – court experiences can range between a single hearing where the case is thrown out to a Crown Court trial that lasts months and months. Expect a crew of Latin-speaking, wig-wearing, posh men to dissect your life as though you're a lab animal. All the while you can't work, get no financial support and no sleep, regardless of innocence or guilt.

Each court discharges to a particular jail so if you're not sure where you'll end up, you can phone the court before-hand and ask them where you're likely to end up. If you're expecting to get jail time then read this book and then give it to your family so you're as prepared as possible, and don't forget to cancel your standing orders and phone contract before you go away or your bank might repossess your life and your phone company will have you in so much debt, you'll need to rob a bank when you get out.

If you're found guilty of a serious crime you might receive what's known as an 'extended sentence' – the judge will give you a minimum term but you may well serve far longer. Getting out is too Kafkaesque to begin to explain here. If you get a fixed term sentence and the judge says two years it likely doesn't mean two years – for this type of sentence you only serve the first half of your sentence inside and if your sentence is less than four years you may be eligible for HDC (Home Detention Curfew house arrest) for part of it.

After prison you'll be released 'on licence' and if you slip up they'll 'recall' you to prison. Eventually you will receive a categorisation (from high – security A-cat to D-cat) but this can take months. More on categorisation in section four of this book.

There are so many exceptions to all of these rules I'm not going to write them all down. I just want you to know that the number the judge reads out often isn't the time you'll actually serve. It can be way more, it can be a bit less.

It's a very good idea to take a 'bang up bag' to court if you think you may end up in prison, more about this can be found in section four. The way courts deal with personal property is a load of C.R.A.P. – you may not be allowed to take anything in the dock, you might be allowed whatever you want. It's a guessing game, but worth a guess nonetheless.

Once you're inside you have to buy items for an extortionate price from your meagre prison wages or have them delivered in to you … long story cut short, it's a headache.

For specific rules about what you can and can't have, look at the particular prisons' 'Local Facilities List' – some are online, some aren't.

TAKING THE PLUNGE

They feed you a lot of custard in jail, so when the judge says 'custody' it's like he's a nineties TV game show host pulling the lever and a whole bathtub of it drops on your head. The yellow slime comes quick so … One quick glance to the gallery and you'll be bundled down to a holding cell.

From court to jail you'll ride in a 'sweat box' – those anonymous-looking white vans that are sweaty during July and freezing cold for the remaining 11 months of the year … the only sweating you'll do is about your predicament. You'll see MAD GAV OV BRUM and TOX09 and LEE 5 YRS 4 GBH RESULT scratched in the paintwork and you'll look at the passing world of freedom through windows that are blacked out so the public needn't see a ne'er-do-well like yourself.

Finally, you'll arrive at the prison gates. They'll flag the van into what's known as 'the sterile area', an officer will shine a torch into your compartment and count you only as a number. Welcome to prison!

You'll step off the bus all wide-eyed. Nineteenth-century prisons look like dilapidated castles, twentieth-century prisons look like broken down leisure centres, and twenty-first century prisons look like Amazon storage warehouses. You'll see big walls, black and white uniforms, one thousand

CCTV cameras and ten thousand pigeons – sounds like I'm describing an average British high street – but understand, the physical appearance makes up only a small part of the psychological control that prison is designed to have over you. I'll say it straight up so you know what you're dealing with: prison is like a monsoon designed to wash away your humanity. These first couple hours in jail are one of the strongest downpours.

You'll be herded to a processing area. Believe me that holding cell is a cocktail of brittle egos at their lowest low. Might be a couple of addicts going through cold turkey puking their guts out, a couple of boys in their 'not-guilty suits' crying their eyes out, a few loose cannons hungry for hierarchy and ready to victimise the 'fraggles' and a good few people totally used to this, like going to jail is easier for them than going to the supermarket. That room is like the waiting room for hell, but hold tight.

A screw will call you by your surname and you'll get processed: you'll be weighed, given a prison number you'll have assigned to you for life, then your belongings will be listed on your property card and you'll be told what

you can have ('IP' – Property In Possession) and largely can't have ('stored property'). Keep a very close eye on exactly what you have in your prop; I had various bits mysteriously disappear, from CDs to my best shirts and brand new trainers that were sent in from outside.

You'll have your photo taken – vain criminals (me) know you have to fix up for the mugshot because that's how you'll forever be remembered. Convicted males get given a scratchy grey tracksuit and pale blue t-shirt, and everyone gets a blue plastic plate and bowl, a plastic knife and fork, mint-green prison issue bed sheets and a dirty orange blanket that has collected dust and pubes from the last decade. You'll also get a 'starter pack' containing milk, tea and sugar. Prisons used to provide basic toiletries (little sachets of greasy shower gel, disposable razors, toothpaste and toothbrushes) but in many institutions you now have to buy these things out of your own pocket; lots of people spend the few quid they have on drugs or instant noodles so get ready for the smell of armpit-mageddon.

Then you'll get searched like you've never been searched before … you'll have to turn around, bend over and cough to make sure you have nothing 'plugged'. Some jails now have airport-style scanners, others have the BOSS (Body Orifice Security Scanner) chair. If they think you're hiding something, you'll be sent straight to the block while they wait for you to do what you've got to do.

You will also see a nurse. They have ten minutes flat to process your entire life through a series of tick boxes on their PC. Self-harm? Drugs? Suicide risk? Allergies? Telling them you're a smoker even if you're not is a good plan – prison is like *Scrapheap Challenge*, take what you can, whenever it's offered. On the other hand, don't even admit to having smoked weed as a kid – like I said, never be honest with a dishonest system. The nurse also selects who gets a single cell and who doesn't – best believe this is a very big deal. Prisoners will be huffing and puffing around, saying, '*I'M A PSYCHO, I SWEAR*' and '*WATCH WHAT WILL HAPPEN IF I DON'T GET A SINGLE CELL*', while the nurse barely looks up at them. Saying you're a bed wetter used to get you a single cell but not any more since jails are completely overcrowded. Your best chance of getting a single cell is to tell them you're hearing voices telling you to strangle your cellmate ... there are long-term implications to trying that route so I wouldn't recommend it.

After this, you'll get moved to the 'first night wing'. You should be allowed to make a free phone call but beware – it only lasts a minute. You should get a shower and you should get bedding but I know a lot of people for whom this hasn't been the case. You'll also need to fill in your first menu sheet – an 'insider' (a prisoner who does jobs for the system) can help with this – if you don't, you'll end up eating 'dis crap' (discrep is the official term for meals left over from the previous day).

*

Other prisoners will be looking you up and down but don't be worried – or at least don't show it – don't be pumped, don't be wet, you should be OK.

In the first week you'll be entitled to a 'reception visit', which is much easier to book than a normal visit. Whoever it is can just call and book to come and see you, they'll just need your date of birth and full name.

You'll get a six-digit pin number for the phone. Make sure you keep it to yourself, otherwise someone can use your credit. Phone numbers have to be approved by the prison and added to your permitted numbers list before you are allowed to ring them, which can take an unreasonably long time (a fortnight or more) so maybe tell your family not to expect to hear from you immediately. By the time it's working, you'll find you've got £2 credit to start off with.

At this point you might be feeling at an all-time mental and physical low – sitting there, overwhelmed by the environment, heavy with anxiety and stress; you often arrive late at the jail and maybe won't have eaten. Plus, if you've got addiction issues you'll be scrambling for nicotine, alcohol, opiates or whatever else. On that note, be cautious of offers from other prisoners, this time of vulnerability is often when people enter the prison debt trap.

If you feel threatened or mentally unstable you can also talk to a prisoner who's specially trained in supporting peers (a Listener); you can also call the Prison Reform Trust freephone advice line (see the Contacts list at the end of this book). I would suggest that the prison system should add my phone number to their list of contacts too – but I'm pretty sure they'll hate my guts by the end of this book.

Something that really helped me was reading other books about people in similar predicaments. *Papillon* by Henri Charrière is about a French guy who was sent to a South American penal colony a hundred years ago. He gets parasites, gets shot, spends years in solitary confinement in a cell that fills up to his neck with water for five hours a day … Reading it all made my shitty situation seem a lot more manageable.

At some point over the next week or two your literacy and numeracy skills will be tested by an Insider or a staff member if there's one available (around half of prisoners have the reading skills of an 11-year-old). You'll also go through induction, where they'll tell you about 'kit change' (getting bed sheets and clothes), the weekly rota, how to get to the library, how to fill in meal slips and some basic and sanitised info about the system: to be honest, by the time you've read this book, you'll be far ahead of the game.

You'll also be assessed by OASys (Offender Assessment System). If you're serving over 12 months determinate they'll give you a 'sentence plan' which will specify the number of days you have to serve (a friend of mine guilty of importing cannabis showed me his and it said 'You will serve 6387 days' ... ouch!). It'll also try to find out why you commit crimes and what the prison system can do for you, which is baffling when the cause of so many crimes is either trauma or poverty, and prison makes you poorer and more damaged. Anyway, they might require you to complete OBPs (Offender Behaviour Programmes. Common ones include CALM – Controlling Anger and Learning to Manage It – and ETS – Enhanced Thinking Skills) and drug treatment programmes.

You might get moved off the induction wing immediately or it might take weeks for the prison to tick their boxes and find you another space in the jail. Whatever happens, the system will start to soak in and I guarantee you'll be shocked. You'll see how inefficient prison is, how much stuff gets thrown over the wall and how easily this could prevent it if the authorities actually wanted to. You'll see how little support is given to illiterate people and drug users when this would stop them reoffending, how many people are rotting away on indefinite sentences when they are ready to be released, how people talk positively about overdosing because it's their only form of escape, how people who don't pay their TV licence get sent to this shithole and then don't have to pay for a TV licence while they're here, how people use ballpoint pens to write haute couture brand names on their tracksuits and smoke teabags wrapped in Bible pages lit with toilet paper and bare cables coming out a plug socket ... and you'll also see how adaptable people are and how many genuinely good-hearted people you end up meeting.

JULIA HOWARD'S STORY

Tears pouring out of my eyes, my face is pressed against the window of the 'sweatbox' as it finally pulls up outside the gates of the prison. I had built up every scenario in my mind: my first thought was that I going to get beaten up upon arrival by either prisoners or staff – or both! I was petrified and had fallen victim to wild and erratic thoughts. By the time I stepped off the van, I was practically hysterical and had no ability for rational thought; the fear was overwhelming and uncontrollable. Looking back now, it was indeed the fear of the unknown and misconceived expectations based on inaccurate judgements and lack of information.

The nineties TV series *Bad Girls* is most people's expectation of female prison. Most of the time it's much more mundane, but sometimes it totally turns into that – the drugs, the chaos and the characters. Some women may even resemble the OTT characters and you think to yourself, 'You must be having a laugh, mate!' You can feel like you're inside a bizarre episode of reality TV, when the TV becomes your reality and your reality is totally surreal.

While men are given a grey tracksuit as standard, women are at least allowed to wear their own clothes. However, I was given three pairs of prison issue knickers – my granny would have been proud of those floral belly-warming numbers!

I also got given prison issue deodorant, tooth brush, toothpaste, hairbrush, sanitary products (pads like nappies and tampons that you fear will give you toxic shock syndrome) and prison issue soap – this stuff is by far the best stain removal product I have ever known, great for cleaning white trainers!

The first prisoners that I came across were the ladies on reception. Unlike the stand-offish male jail dynamic Carl mentions, the female prisoners I met in reception brought me a cup of tea and were really kind and comforting. They were just normal people, just like me and you. Some staff on reception were at times very rude and abrupt, others were very helpful – in fact, some of the staff fitted my preconceived expectations more than the prisoners. There is good and bad in every walk of life and this is no different 'behind the wall'.

I was taken over to the first night centre but I was still hysterical and I could feel my mental health spiralling. This is when I was most vulnerable. I really did just want the ground to swallow me up – I didn't care if I lived or died in that moment. It is easy to see why, between 2010 and 2016, there was a 1,200 per cent increase in suicides in prison.

Please believe me, it does get easier: just be strong and get through the first night, first week, first month and you will look back and see how far you have come. It's OK not to be OK, so don't be too hard on yourself.

THE JAIL ENVIRONMENT

Put a bunk bed in your toilet and invite a random person off the street to come stay for six months and you'll start to understand cell life.

Every jail is different (C.R.A.P. really does apply!) but it'll be something like the following: nine foot long by six foot wide, a wall-mounted cabinet and a battered little wooden unit with a TV sat on top, in one corner a sink and toilet (you best look the other way and put a clothes peg on your nose if you're sharing the cell).

Expect a bed that creaks with every fidget, a plastic mattress and pillow with the prison issue bedding I already described. Newer prisons have bright white clean walls with a halogen electric light that makes you feel like a lab rat, old prisons have sodium lights that make you feel like you're living in a grow house. Some people hate the graffiti on the walls but I liked it because it was the most human element ... Payper On Tour 2015, detailed drawings of AK-47s, in-depth conspiracy theories, disturbing diagrams about the Holocaust and 'I'M A CELEBRITY GET ME OUT OF HERE – TAFFY OF NORTH WALES'.

One end of the cell there's a window, with thick metal bars, of course. Sometimes there will be a skinny panel that

you can open for ventilation and other times there's this kind
of perforated sheet metal, where you have to turn a knob to
open or close. I was in multiple cells where I couldn't close
the window and ended up using jail-issue toothpaste to stick
scraps of cardboard over the window to stop the frost. In a
lot of jails the heating comes in the form of a big heated
pipe that runs through the whole building. At the other end
of the cell, there's a massive door with an observation flap
only openable from the outside, with a tiny pinhole for surveillance – screws can try to be sly, but you'll be able to see
the shadows of their boots if you're looking out for them.
The door is filled with concrete and weighs a ton.

Stepping outside of your cell you'll find the wing like
a big hall. Ground-floor landings are known as 'the 1s'
(pronounced 'ones'), the next floor is 'the 2s', then the
'3s' and so on. Prisoners with wing jobs and prisoners
on Enhanced (those with greater privileges) generally
live on the 1s. That's also where you'll normally find the
staff office, the meds (medical) hatch, the servery and the
gates to leave the wing, maybe a pool table. There will
also be CCTV cameras that won't catch much, as it's very
obvious where they see and where they don't.

To prevent prisoners jumping to their deaths there are
anti-suicide nets commonly known as chip nets. If you
don't know, chip is slang for leaving, and the net stops
you from leaving, if you know what I mean.

The day begins with 'unlock' at around 8am. It's like waiting
for walkies: you'll hear the doors being unlocked down the
hall, coming slowly closer to you before it's your time, then
you're out of the cell and it's noisy and chaotic straight off
the bat. Get a cup of tea and a bit of breakfast, then at
9am the wing gates open for people to go on 'moves'.

'Moves' (also known as 'free flow') is the ten minute
period where you can transfer between different areas
of the prison. The place is full of mesh fences, temporary buildings and outbuildings, all crenellated with razor
wire to keep you where they want you. Staff will stand by

the gates that separate the units and tick you off as you leave or enter.

The day is divided into sessions, each 'sesh' is an hour and a half. At 10.30am, the first session is over and mid-morning moves commence. Another hour and a half and it's midday moves, where everyone except for kitchen staff have to return to the wing for lunch.

After getting food you're banged up for an hour or so while staff go to their own canteen. I've never watched so much daytime TV – honestly, that stuff makes *Emmerdale* look like it could win an Oscar.

At around 1pm you'll be unlocked and sent off to the next sesh or locked back in your cell. At 2.30pm it's mid-afternoon moves, then it's 4pm and everyone comes back to the wing. Teatime is seriously early; in my experience by 5pm I was often locked up for the night ready for six waking hours of cage. Some jails have evening 'sosh' (association time, or social time) but this has been curtailed since prisons lost so many staff.

The dirt and the smells of prison are foul. Out the window of HMP Wormwood Scrubs I could see David Cameron's multi-million pound house, then I'd look down on the floor and see these prehistoric parasites called silverfish. Expect cockroaches, families of rats living in piles of rubbish in the yards, rotting pigeons caught in the netting, decomposing fruit hanging around longer than most prisoners.

The sounds of jail seep into the fabric of your mind over the months and years. It's clattering chaos from the minute you are unlocked – shouting, banging doors, tinkling keys … all echoing and bouncing. There are no carpets, no soft anything, everything in prison is tinny and hard. I actually made a documentary called *Sounds Inside* for NPR (National Prison Radio) – it's on my website – go check it out if you want to hear more of the jail soundscape.

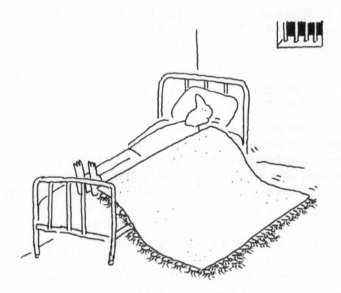

Kicking the door is a nationwide prison tradition. Prisoners 'bang the door' whenever something noteworthy happens; when someone escapes the police on *CrimeWatch* (RIP *CrimeWatch*, 1984–2017, you will be sorely missed by prisoners), when someone gets laid on reality TV, when Arsenal get a hat trick against Tottenham … in prison you can tell the football score without even watching the TV. The yearly pinnacle of doorbanging is New Year's Eve: every single person in the jail up and down the country absolutely kicks the shit out of their door.

You can tune in to NPR on your cell TV. It's great. They have programmes ranging from the *Travellers Talk Show* to a yoga and mindfulness show, and loads of music stuff in between. You can write into their request line and dedicate it to someone, as a prisoner or as someone outside, but unfortunately you can only hear it inside currently.

Also worth a mention is that pirate radios transmit messages for people in London prisons. Pirate radio is proper community radio, it's no wonder they want to take them off the airwaves. Tune into Kool FM and occasionally you'll hear things like 'Carl on Scrubs B–Wing your sister is stuck in traffic, she won't make the visit and is very sorry!'

CELL MATES

Prison and privacy are two words that share the first three letters, but they have no overlap whatsoever: you're constantly watched by guards you hate, you share a cell and showers with people you've never met and your phone calls, letters and most private information are monitored by people you will never meet.

So Let's talk about cellmates. To state the obvious, the kind of person you share a cell with will have a massive impact on your existence.

Don't enter the cell, plonk your stuff down and just change the TV channel, and don't sit on anyone else's bed without invitation. People who've been in jail the longest or in the cell the longest have a presumed seniority but if you just show you're going to be easy to work with then they'll work easier with you – mutual respect diffuses most macho bullshit, that tiny little box is not a place for being a territorial dickhead.

My first cellmate become a really good friend but I also shared with eyebrowless Russians who didn't speak a word of English besides racist insults, a grumpy old bank robber who just farted and smoked fags on the bunk below me all day and, for one night only, an addict going full cold turkey: shitting and puking all night in the toilet situated just at the end of the bed – between every spew, he looked up and apologised profusely for keeping me awake. Not having NASA (Nice And Safe Armpits) can be a definite conflict point between cellmates. This issue has no doubt deteriorated since they stopped giving out free shower gel.

Arguments do happen, mostly about the TV. It's such a big part of prison life that if you don't have similar taste

then it will become a point of conflict. Reminds me of when I was a teenager and I wanted to watch *Neighbours* at 5.30pm but my little brother wanted to watch *Pet Rescue* instead. I really hated him for it and I'm not even sure if I'm over it yet. It's basically this situation times one hundred. If you like reading then ask around, and try and find someone who's not square-eyed.

Another point of conflict comes if you're trying to keep it clean (no phone and no drugs) and you end up sharing with someone who's doing dirt, because if something is found in the cell, both people will get charged unless one person admits it's theirs, which is unlikely. For this reason, people who are doing stuff often share with a Joey (a subservient, addicted or destitute prisoner), who will take the possession charge, either paid with drugs or forced with threats. So if your release depends on good behaviour then I'd get out of that cell ASAP, by any means possible.

Putting your foot down and not getting treated like shit will make your life easier in the long run. But fighting with the person you share a cell with is hell on earth so if your cellmate is being a nightmare then move before it kicks off. Don't snitch to staff, just keep it calm until you can get out. I never had these problems but I did change cell to be with mates; personally I didn't do it by application because this rarely achieves anything. Just get your possessions bagged up, persuade your friend's current cellmate to move (a can of tuna or two will smooth out the deal) and just do it. Tell the screws it's already happened and they should be OK with it (but don't blame me if they're not). This is quite often how it works in prison – if you go through the correct channels, you get nowhere. Just get on with it, be confident and use initiative and you'll be fine. Hopefully.

Now you've heard about sharing a cell, you'll probably understand why being single-cell is so highly coveted. I'd still prefer it even if the distilled loneliness you can go through is something that most people will never experience in their life. I did ten months in 23-hour lock-up and it changed my personality forever. But I'd still prefer it to sharing with someone I don't know.

FOOD

You'll choose what you want for lunch and dinner from a menu sheet at the beginning of each week. There might be four options per day with at least one halal and one vegetarian choice. The idea of a big mess hall where everyone eats off metal trays was definitely not my experience: in the UK, you go with your baby blue plastic plate, queue up, collect your slop and get herded back to your cell.

Prisons currently have budgets of between £1.15 and £2.10 per day per prisoner, so expect small portions of crap food … gritty burgers, disinfectant-flavoured rice,

sugary baked beans, quadruple-microwaved chicken and sponge cake covered with sticky custard. The tiny portions are bolstered by bread. Lots and lots of shit bread, which smells a bit like clothes left in the washing machine for too long.

Unless opiates, ganja and spice count as fruit and veg, then virtually no one is getting their five a day. Expect no salad, very little fresh fruit and vegetables overcooked until they're mush. Yo, Jamie Oliver, where you at?

Breakfast comes in the form of a plastic bag that contains ultra-strong teabags (aka diesel), a carton of UHT milk, coffee whitener and various types of cereal depending on the day. You know people call prison 'doing porridge', really it should be called 'doing choco Rice Krispies' because no one goes near the porridge sachets, so if you let people know that you like porridge, you'll get avalanched with these mini-packs of oats until you're released.

If you are diabetic or have any other dietary requirements you should be given a supplementary pack every

day, which will probably be of less little benefit to your condition but might mean you get extra milk or some fruit(!); just let the staff know that you need it when you first get on the wing, then complain until you finally get it.

A perk of a kitchen job is selling bits and bobs to prisoners back on the wing, these might help you liven up your food a bit. Pepper and spices are disallowed in a lot of jails because people would blow it in screws' eyes – I used to laugh to myself when I was stashing black pepper in my mattress like it's some kind of Class A drug.

You can also make some simple recipes from the bits available in the canteen (if you have the money and IEP status) to make prison grub slightly more edible. Here are a few suggestions …

INSTANT NOODLES WITH TUNA

A prison staple, the best meal you'll get inside. Order both off the canteen.

BAKED BEANS ON TOAST

* Throw the complete can in the kettle then open it once it's properly warmed up.

* Wrap bread in a piece of newpaper and stick it on the hot pipes for five minutes. Less 'toast', more dried-out bread, but you'll survive.

SALAD DRESSING

* Take an empty ketchup bottle.
* Two parts sunflower oil from a can of tuna.

* One part vinegar given out in sachets or available on canteen.
* Mix in lots of mixed herbs, pepper, salt, chili sauce, mustard or brown sauce, whatever you can get hold of.
* Shake well and that's that.

KETTLE CURRIES & DUMPLINGS

HMP kettle cooking is like going on a dystopian camping trip. You can get tinned fish and various other bits off the canteen, but cooking it takes a bit of a knack because there is only one setting on a kettle: turbo heat or nothing.

YOGHURT

My Albanian mates made amazing yoghurt in their cells from prison issue UHT milk. Google says this isn't even possible, but I saw it live and kicking. You'll have to ask them if you want to know how they do it.

PRISONOMICS

A lot of people come to jail when their get-rich-quick scheme doesn't go to plan but then the irony is that in jail, you earn about a fiver a *week* and you never even touch hard currency.

Let me just repeat – a fiver a week – prisoners haven't received a pay rise since 1997 back when 1p sweets cost 1p. To supplement your income you have to rely on money being sent in, but this shouldn't be taken for granted because many prisoners do not get any external support whatsoever.

To get money sent in the options include postal orders (very expensive), cash (gets stolen) or cheques (slow). If you're sending them to someone inside, make cheques and postal orders payable to H M Prison Service and write your name, the prisoner's full name and prison number on the back of the envelope. In public prisons you can transfer through the Ministry of Justice website. £20 is so appreciated – money that is small change on the outside can be the most solid way to support a prisoner.

Way before my time prisons had an actual canteen, like a little village store. But, like the village shop, it has now been replaced by a DHL mail order. The only thing that remains is the name. So once every week a two-sided A4 'canteen sheet' gets slipped under your door. On the top of the sheet it'll tell you how much you have in your 'privates' and 'spends'.

'Privates' is the account where people send money to. 'Spends' is the amount you can actually spend that week – this amount is defined by your IEP status and your wage. You get £2.50 'bang up money' absolutely free; you have to pay £1 rent for your TV (the Ministry of Justice make £500,000 a year off this).

The predictable connivances happen. 'Enchanted ones' (prisoners on Enhanced Status who have larger spends) will charge an inflated price to put bits for others on their canteen spend and get money transferred externally – the rich get richer, even in prison.

The canteen sheet will show all the various bits available, from batteries to Bounty bars to phone credit. When you've got ten quid for the entire week it's a bit like being a 1950s housewife: you will spend hours pondering, 'Can I justify spending 60p on a chocolate bar or should I spend it all on phone credit, or should I put half on phone credit and half towards the new pillowcase I want to buy in three months … ?' Make your mind up and put the quantity next to the item you want and (very important) highlight or circle it as they often get missed.

Your items will be delivered a few days later in a sealed clear plastic bag, normally while you're on lunchtime bang up. It's like Christmas except that Santa is dressed in a grey trackie. Don't open the bag until you've checked the contents – if you thought that getting robbed by a vending machine for a chocolate bar was bad, then try getting robbed by a sheet of paper for the only instant noodles you'll have for a week.

Bigger bits and pieces like clothes and stereos are available only from approved suppliers. The list of available products should be available from the wing office. It changes in every jail but they're generally Argos, DHL, Sports Direct and a few catalogues that were made obsolete by the QVC Shopping Channel around the Millennium (check the Facilities List for your jail, if one is available). The strict rules around suppliers are justified on the basis of security – so people can't send in drugs or extremist literature – but the reality is that it prevents financially squeezed prisoners and their families sending in stuff bought cheaply and means they have to buy it new from these lot.

When supplier contracts are put out to tender the winner is the company who can provide the cheapest service to the Ministry of Justice, not the company who can provide goods cheapest to the prisoner. Prisonomics isn't economical for prisoners.

If you're up for a good time then have a look at this website – www.contractsfinder.service.gov.uk – and search for prison. Check out what's currently up for grabs. When I last checked (in October 2018), you could get £7m for supplying electrical appliances including in-cell kettles – I wonder if the businessman knows what he's letting himself in for; I wonder if he's ever used a cell kettle to cook instant noodle tuna masala.

JOBS

Human Rights Act Article 4: Freedom From Slavery And Forced Labour does not apply to prisons: work is compulsory for convicted adult prisoners. If you have pride and refuse to work, you'll get put on Basic, which will mean one visit a month and no TV.

Prison jobs include being a wing cleaner, an orderly (for education department, library, church or wherever else), a

'womble' (a litter picker), a wing rep (the on-wing representative of a prison department), a wing painter, a gardener,
or a visit room cleaner. One of the best paid of these jobs
is a 'biohazard' (a prisoner that cleans up other prisoners'
blood puke and faeces).

A full-time job is considered to be ten sessions a week,
around the 40 hours mark, like a full-time job on The Out.
The major difference is the wage ... the minimum wage
in prison is £4 per week. By my own estimation I'd say
the average wage is about a tenner a week but apparently, they do go all the way up to £50ish if you're working
high up for a private contractor in an outside environment,
which is possible in some prisons ... but listen, those
high-paying jobs are virtually non-existent.

   If you get paid £5 a week then a jail Pepperami costs
16 per cent of your wages, a pack of jail Gillette razors
costs 80 per cent, a pack of KP Nuts will set you back
25 per cent ... it's nuts. What's even more nuts is that
a ten-minute call to a UK mobile phone (about 20p per
minute) will cost you 40 per cent of your entire weekly
wage!

   If you are too sick to work you'll get a measly £2.50
a week for the first four weeks and £3.25 every week for
every week thereafter. Disabled prisoners receive £8.50 a
week. If you're on a state pension you won't receive it while
you're inside, regardless of whether or not other people in
your family are dependent on it, but if you're on a private
pension (and likely more wealthy), you'll still receive it.

An undisclosed number of private companies take
advantage of cheap prison labour in the UK. While DHL
describes working in its prison warehouses as a 'meaningful experience', we call the prison warehouses 'noddy
shops' or 'hobbit shops' because the jobs – separating
wires, counting washers, even assembling those little red
poppies for Remembrance Day – are so completely mind-
numbing, you feel like a little gremlin.

Don't get confused: they're in the prison system for the profits. They pay prisoners the same amount for a week's work as they would pay an external employee in an hour. This whole scheme is known as the 'prison industrial complex' and people should really know more about it – read Angela Davis's excellent work for the full low-down.

In terms of unpaid work, there are worthy volunteer positions, like being a Listener, an Insider or a Toe By Toe mentor. I was the latter; it's a great scheme where you teach prisoners to read and write in your cell. I taught a born-and-bred Londoner who couldn't read the word *cat* … I bumped into him in another prison and he was almost tearful, telling me how he could now write letters to his daughter. If you can't read then I doubt you'll be reading this, but Toe By Toe mentors wear red t-shirts with the Toe By Toe logo – staff can point you in their direction.

Insiders are in an interesting position. To become one you have to be recommended by the wing staff and then appointed by a wing governor. They (are supposed to) do all the menial stuff that staff formerly did – answering basic questions about how to get stuff done, providing another dirty blanket because the window won't shut maybe getting you a compassionate phone call if you're grieving. They run the induction course in some prisons and even do the literacy and numeracy assessments. They also serve as a sort of MP as they have regular meetings with governors; they can directly complain about the cold showers, the cockroaches and whatever else isn't up to scratch (not sure if it helps, judging by the state of things). Insiders are 'trusted prisoners' aka Red Bands so they get no love from prisoners who see them as skivvies for 'the others'.

CURRENCY

If you just read the previous chapter it's not hard to see why people have their little side hustles in HMP. When legitimate economies are made impossible, people become black marketeers, that's just how it goes. Tobacco used to be the unit of currency until it was banned very recently and so, wistfully, I tell you that gone are the days of 'Barons' sitting there with stacks of Golden Virginia like it was gold bullion. The nouveau Barons stack tins of fish and toiletries so high you can't see out the cell window.

It's a bit like living in Asterix & Obelix's village – everyone has their own little enterprise. Kitchen workers will smuggle you some black pepper or herbs in exchange for a tin or two of tuna. The laundry and stores lot will make sure your clothes actually get clean in return for an energy drink. The guy in charge of kit-change will make sure you get bed sheets that aren't totally covered in pubes if you give him some instant noodles. Hairdressers make a killing (a killing of tuna and shower gel) because everyone wants to look prim with a fresh trim for their visit – I'd advise buying clippers and becoming a wing barber but be

warned: you might get into tuna-based territorial conflict (no joke).

Then there are medium-value items. The local artiste will draw you a birthday card, a love letter or a get well soon card. The craftsmen will build you a set of drawers from matchsticks and glue. Hooch costs around £10 per litre depending on the quality.

Expensive bits like drugs, tobacco (50g currently costs around £500!) or buying a stereo off someone will be paid for beyond the prison walls. The buyer's friend on The Out will pay the seller's friend on The Out and once payment is received, the item will be handed over.

In fact, some people come to prison just to make money or pay off debts. They'll swallow as many drugs as possible then intentionally get arrested in order to sell the drugs on the wing. This lifestyle is more bizarre the more you think about it: no one does this shit unless they truly need to (or are forced to).

DEBT

On The Out there are payday loan shops, bookies, and banks, and the prison equivalent are the Barons, who lend money using a scheme known as Double Bubble. It's as it sounds – you borrow something (drugs/nicotine patches/painkillers/food/toiletries) then repay double the next week. If you can't manage the payback, you might enter a debt spiral where you are forced to pay back more and more and more.

The induction wing is the hotspot for this stuff because this is where people are at their most strung out, their least well–provisioned (waiting a week or two for their first canteen, and that's if they have money) and their most innocent.

I mean, a lot of people borrow and do manage to pay it back, but if you can't you'll end up in a bad way. Beaten up, fingers slammed in a cell door, or you might become a Joey.

In extreme cases people get themselves put on cucumbers (or numbers, the Vulnerable Persons Unit) or try to move prisons, but Barons aren't stupid: debtors are required to give family details and families are targeted if the debtor gets out of reach.

Whilst high street money businesses legally use bailiff thugs in uniform, Barons do the same with boys in trackies: truth be told, the difference isn't that big.

You never see loan shops in a posh area, do you – desperation necessitates debt so some random author saying 'Hey, don't borrow money!' is totally patronising. All I'm saying is know what you're dealing with. If you're really in a debt pickle you can call Stop Loan Sharks on 0300 555 2222, free from the wing payphone.

IEP SYSTEM

The Incentive Earned Privileges system is cruel and divisive – it is designed to encourage prisoners to behave however it's so badly thought out that it often has exactly the opposite effect.

You'll get an IEP warning if you break minor prison rules – for example if you wear flip flops on the landing, turn up late to work or swear in the presence of a staff member. These warnings then affect your IEP level. In the short term this dictates what clothes you can wear, how much time you can spend out of your cell, how many visits you receive, how much money you have access to. In the long term this can all affect your likelihood of being recategorised, given Release On Temporary License, or being granted freedom by a parole board. Check it out – the big old snakes and ladders game of IEP ...

Entry is where you'll find yourself when you're new to the establishment, regardless of whether you're on remand, recall, serving your fifteenth sentence or if you've just been transferred from another jail. On Entry, convicted prisoners have potential access to £10 'spends', unconvicted prisoners have £35, plus any wages, sickness pay or pension. To 'progress' you need to have completed induction (it wasn't even available a lot of the time in my experience), show 'willingness to engage with work', do education, addiction treatment programmes and behaviour management courses. And if all goes well for 14 days you'll get put on:

Standard, where it's largely the same except convicted spends rise to £15.50 and unconvicted £47.50. And if all goes well for three months you'll be eligible for:

Enhanced. Convicted spends rise to £25.50, unconvicted £51. You can wear your own garms and you get four hours visiting time a month (the maximum possible). Also you have to consistently display your willingness to be part of the system – this includes having 'an exemplary relationship with staff' and 'engaging in schemes that helps prisoners and officers' (for example, being a Listener, Buddy, Toe By Toe mentor or Wing Representative). Prisoners on Enhanced are known as 'the enchanted ones' (not necessarily a compliment).

Basic. This is where you'll end up if you get three IEP warnings. You'll have much less time out of your cell (how's that's even possible in these days of 23-hour bang up?), no evening association and you'll have your TV taken away. Your spends are reduced to £4 convicted and £22 unconvicted, you have limited access to education and resettlement opportunities. Finally, your visits are limited to just two hours a month.

This is a punishment for your family as much as for you. Family contact is proven to increase the chance of rehabilitation and resettlement and reduce reoffending; they punish you by taking away the things that give you stability and purpose. The irony is that it's non-compliant prisoners who are often the most in need of more of these things, not less!

Access to a TV may seem like a minor thing, but the sad reality is that in prison it's a major one – it's like a surrogate family for some and plugs the void of meaningful activity. When it's taken away, it can lead to people becoming a bigger risk to themselves and to others.

The IEP system is basically a microcosm of the entire justice system. Prisoners with pride don't jump through hoops, they just ride Basic for their whole sentence. The architects of this system don't understand the first thing about the people they're dealing with.

It's one thing if you're serving a determinate sentence, it's a whole different thing if you're serving an 'extended sentence': IEP warnings can prevent you from being released: prisoners in for a violent crime who haven't been aggressive towards anyone (within that stupidly aggressive environment – major challenge) can be denied release for an infraction.

IEP also limits your access to finances. Firstly, people get in debt. Secondly, not everyone has family who can put £200 a month into your prison account. If you don't have that money coming in then there's even less incentive to abide by the IEP system.

Basic regime is totally overused and totally ineffective. In fact, the percentage of prisoners on Basic increased by 52 per cent between 2012 and 2014.

Cough, cough, Ministry of Justice ... People have been saying this for yeeaarrs, this system must be fixed ASAP.

STAFF MEMBERS

Prison officers or screws (aka Scoobies, The Who, kangas – as in kangaroos). There are three main types you need to know about: your personal officer who will know slightly more about your case, general wing officers and, lastly, senior officers. Really though, there's only one type of screw – the type that needs to be kept at arm's length. Old cockney boys call the authorities The Other Lot – this slang is so on point, it tells you all you need to know. Treating a screw as a friend is a very bad idea because firstly, you'll get labelled a 'screw-boy' i.e. a teacher's pet, secondly, within a professional capacity the screws have no loyalty to you whatsoever – forget their personality, just look at their uniform, the keys to your liberty that hang from their belts, their bodyworn camera (anything you do say may be used against you) and their taser guns (self-explanatory).

Despite me telling you this, you will probably lapse into a sort of friendship at some point – for months or even years you'll spend far more time with them than your family – but then the most minor thing and they'll nick you, send you to the block, or write a report about you that prevents you from getting parole or early release.

At the same time, don't go out of your way to piss screws off because they'll go further out of their way to do the same to you and remember, they have the keys; in multiple senses. Smile to their face and keep it sweet, but like I said, remember that they are 'The Other Lot'.

In one way I feel really sorry for them. Prisoners hate the system and get treated like dirt, prison officers are loyal to the system and get treated largely the same! We both serve sentences. It's a gnarly job as far as physical and mental health goes.

Before funding cuts, the screws used to have time to talk to prisoners and sense the dynamic, plus they'd have a decent staff canteen and overtime pay or whatever else. But now they get attacked all the time (attacks on staff rose 26 per cent from 2017–18 alone), paid a terrible wage and are surrounded by an ever-worsening atmosphere of self-harm, suicide and drug use. I used to sit there in my cell at night-time imagining the officers driving back home, looking at the rain on their windscreen, thinking about cutting dead prisoners down from the lights and rescuing people from overdoses like, 'What the fuckkkkk did I just see at work today?!' Anyone who passes through this environment will be mentally damaged: soldiers get lacklustre support and they're considered heroes so I doubt prison officers get the support they need either. Prison officers with bad mental health are good news for absolutely no one.

Many experienced officers have left the service for the above reasons and are being replaced by kids, some of whom were literally stacking supermarket shelves the week before. The newbies simply don't know who's who and what's what. It's a bit like having a supply teacher: no work gets done, they don't know the dynamic, the naughty kids just run rings round them.

Providing these underpaid, overworked, new-to-the-game screws with bodycams, taser guns and instant coffee provides no answers, just more problems. Lisa Selby (who writes on page 90) says that these new officers seem to make up for their lack of training and experience by imitating the way 'correctional facilities officers' do the job on American TV shows.

When things predictably get out of hand (currently, a dozen times a week) the prison calls in the NTRG (National Tactical Response Group) aka the turbo-screws, and when a riot kicks off, you'll meet the 'tornado team' aka turbo-GTI-screws. Each T-team consists of 50 or so specially trained meatlump officers dressed head to toe in black with riot shields, helmets and taser guns. There's a good chance you'll see them as there are almost three times more prison riots today than there were a decade ago.

DST (Dedicated Search Teams) win the award for my favourite bit of prison slang – we call them the Burglars because they come to your cell and take your favourite stuff. They are a separate unit with specialist knowledge and equipment. The funny thing is the screws often dislike them too because they investigate the staff as well. Which brings me on to Corrupt officers, aka 'cons with keys'. There are estimated to be three or so in every jail. Anyone who's on things will know which member of staff to talk to.

There are a lot of other people working in the prison – probation officers, pen pushers, and contractors.

Above the Senior Officer on the wing is a Principal Officer who communicates directly with Governors. There are various 'grades' of Governor – you'll see them on the wing from time to time, dressed in suits rather than black and white uniforms, you'll also meet them if you get a nicking. Above them all is the number one Governor, who runs the prison.

The organisational structure of the MoJ seems totally abstract when you're on the wing but for completion, I'll explain it in brief: HMPPS (Her Majesty's Prison and Probation Service) operate the whole lot from start to finish. The top bods are the Prisons Minister and the Justice Minister, but I won't name either because they don't hang around very long. They're based at the Ministry of Justice, which isn't a very apt name for it. Their HQ in central London is worth a look – it's like a malevolent concrete brutalist spaceship that has come to abduct your friends.

SECURITY

Security measures in prison range from a standard cell 'spin' (search) by dud wing screws to the burglars locking off the whole wing and searching every cell with dogs.

Screws used to boast with glee that 'nobody beats the BOSS' but they weren't ready for the Zanco Fly phone. This phone is described by consumers as being the best bumphone on the market. Not only does it have virtually no plastic components, but it's also the size of a thumb, which is an improvement on a BlackBerry, if you know what I mean.

If the BOSS detects something then you have to 'produce it' or they will hold you in the block until you ditch it – you can either flush it away or do the two-toilet-transfer.

Once you're on the wing you might meet the Burglars. If they come for you, good luck. Whether it's hidden in the

light fixing, in one of those little compartments made of toothpaste behind noticeboards, behind a false wall in a jewellery box, round the toilet U-bend or up your arse. All these techniques are old hat.

People on the wing always said you get searched *more* if you're not using or selling drugs because it suits them to not find anything ... I guess it would make sense as that way the staff would have less paperwork, the system looks as though it's doing good and the government has to provide less funding for drug treatment courses. Great news for people who are up to stuff, it's bad news for drug addiction levels and terrible news for people who will end up being victims of crimes solely committed to fund addictions that weren't solved or were acquired behind bars. If you keep getting spun then maybe plant some-thing on yourself just to prank them (please, that's a joke ... don't do that).

Remember, there are many other ways to let the screws know you're up to something: if you buy ten batteries each week, they will know you're charging a mobile phone. If you talk about mobile phones over the blue box (wing payphone), you are a total idiot. And to state the obvious, they're trained in slang (they might even add this book to the training course). So you need to up your game ... old school gypsy 'cant' slang was highly developed to stop authorities understanding a word, new school London slang like zamera, rambo and opps sucks because it can be worked out in one minute flat, it's fuck-ing useless.

Oh, and, if you're on remand for a serious crime there are the visit room lip readers who will be keeping an eye on you. It's rumoured that officers have also been known to have highly illegal roots through unconvicted prisoners' legal documents while they're away from their cells then report back the details to prosecution lawyers. If you have sensitive documents in your cell, maybe get friends to look after them while you're off the wing at work or a visit.

GETTING A NICKING

If you do something really silly, you will be arrested within the prison, taken to a criminal court and potentially given another sentence. But if you do something only a little bit silly, you'll get a 'nicking'. This is where you're put through the adjudication process, the prison's internal justice system.

Here are some examples: you are not allowed to pos-sess chewing gum, an 18-rated film or a mobile phone. You are not allowed to brew hooch, be mouthy, borrow

books from another prisoner or test positive for a banned substance.

An officer has to give you two forms within 48 hours of the occurrence: the first (DIS1, or a 'nicking sheet') will explain what you've done wrong and the second (DIS2) explains what will happen next. Overleaf you can write a written statement or request the presence of witnesses. As with the police I'd recommend giving no comment until you've got proper advice and the situation has cooled down.

For more serious charges, such as possession of a mobile phone or a proper assault, you will face an 'Independent Adjudication' by a visiting judge. In this instance you can get legal aid and, as ever, when it's available, I'd strongly recommend you take it.

For more minor charges you will face a 'Governors Adjudication'. You can call witnesses (prisoners or members of staff) but you should ask them before getting them involved. You can't get legal aid despite the fact that, if you're found guilty, it can impact your recategorisation, ROTL (release on temparary licence) and eventual freedom. I'd strongly recommend calling the Prisoner's Advice Service (PAS) on their freephone advice line in this situation. You can also call the Howard League's advice line if you are under 21. You should also read the Prison Discipline Manual (aka PSI 47/2011) and really take your time to study this … two hours spent reading mind-numbing legal drear might mean you find that the screws failed one tiny guideline and therefore your nicking will be dismissed on technicalities.

For proper legal representation you have to pay, and for most this isn't an option however you can still use a 'McKenzie Friend'. They are an odd facet of English and Welsh law (it's slightly different in Scotland and Northern Ireland) which allows a McKenzie Friend to sit with you, read documents and provide advice even though they can't represent you. It can be a friend, a fellow prisoner or an unpaid solicitor. For more information see www.mckenzie-friend.org.uk.

As PAS, the Howard League and the manual will explain, you have a right to see all paperwork relating to the charge before the adjudication starts so be sure to ask for it.

The adjudication itself: in my experience it is like a hybrid of police station and school. The Governor sits there like the headmaster (more Demon Headmaster than Dumbledore) then hears the grumbles from both you (defendant) and the prison officers (prosecution witnesses).

In an external court, the police and judges are a separate entity, but in prison, the Governor serves as judge, prosecution lawyer, court clerk and manager who has got to keep his staff (the prison officers) happy. Cockney rhyming slang for a screw is kanga, so can you guess what these courts are known as?

Sorry, I'm getting distracted. Once you're in the hearing, you will get asked a bunch of questions (which are more for the system to cover it's arse than for you to get a fair chance). Question number five is always 'Do you want legal advice or representation during the hearing before proceeding further?' – this is your best chance of adjourning the case and maybe even derailing it. The prison has a legal duty to help you locate other prisoners who may have witnessed an incident, even if you have no idea of their name or appearance. You can also ask to see CCTV from the wing.

At all points make sure the adjudicator writes all requests, agreements, refusals and reasoning down in case you later need to rely on them.

Then the judgement: if you're found guilty, the punishment can include any of the following …

- You might be prevented from accessing funds (for a maximum of 84 days), which means fewer noodles, less shower gel and less phone credit to call your family.
- You can get put on Basic (one visit a month, no TV).
- You can receive a suspended sentence that can cover any of the above but will only activate if you commit another offence within its duration.
- You can be put on closed visits (where there's a sheet of Perspex between you and your visitors).
- You can receive a maximum of 42 extra days for each offence (extra days can only be given at Independent Adjudication). You can't get extra days if you're Extended Sentence but the nicking will definitely affect your likelihood of ever being released.
- Getting sent to the block (aka seg, segregation, cellular confinement, the dungeon or chokey) for up to one month. The official name for the block is the Care and Separation unit, which is about as accurate as calling the Ministry of Justice the Ministry of Justice. I was in the block while waiting for my adjudication hearing; it was a cold cell with cold-hearted staff, no TV, no stimulation, an overwhelming atmosphere of self-harm. To paraphrase a government report on HMP Bedford: catching rats is the only productive thing you can do in that place. If I was being dramatic, I'd say seg is like the death penalty for your soul; if I was being real, I'd say prisoners go in and out of it like it's no worries. I wish it upon no one except maybe the authorities responsible for it still

being a legally permissible punishment in a developed country in the twenty-first century. An even worse version of this punishment is the Strip Cell, where you're not even permitted to wear clothes, only out-nastied by CSCs, or Close Supervision Centres. Down the block *everything* is either fixed to the walls or floor to prevent them from being used as weapons against self or staff. When I was there the block was full of mentally ill prisoners who were howling. While in the block you should have access to the phone, shower and exercise yard but due to understaffing, you will be lucky if these are a daily occurrence. The only people you'll see are seg officers, the occasional governor or medic and the seg orderly (a prisoner who does stuff like bring you food). You can still request to see a Listener and I'd advise doing that if you're feeling topsy-turvy – a lot of people commit suicide down the block. They might even put you in a body belt (a newfangled straitjacket) – a belt with handcuffs attached that is reserved for people who are seriously kicking off.

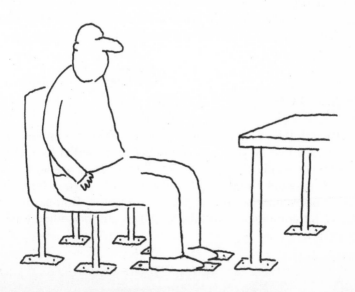

To appeal: for a Governor's Adjudication, you submit a form DIS8 within six weeks of the conclusive hearing. If this is unsuccessful you can elevate it to the Prison and Probation Ombudsman within three months. For an Independent Adjudication, you fill in an IA4 form and submit it within the 14-day time limit.

Sounds complex? It is. I haven't even included the whole fiddle. For the full lowdown, see the Prison Reform Trust document about prison rules, the government's Prison Service Orders and Prison Service Instructions or the Prison Handbook, which should be available from the prison library.

Can I interrupt myself to say I knew *none* of this when I was going through adjudications and was simply never told a shred of this. Before someone says it, yes, I'm sure the details were buried in small print but I had no knowledge of resources available and no idea of the significance of being found guilty. If you combine prison levels of illiteracy, mental health issues, drug addiction and lack of legal aid, it's a pretty bitter old cocktail. It should come as no surprise to you that two-thirds of people are found guilty at adjudication. This all leads me on to the obvious – if you are behind bars and are a small print warlord, then offer your help to others – it can have a massive impact on their future freedom.

COMPLAINTS AND APPLICATIONS

To get things done you'll need to rely on paperwork. Somewhere on your wing there will be a load of forms that have been photocopied so many times they are light grey and so wonky that they're falling off the page. There are job applications, property hand out forms, Comps (which are for complaints) and Apps (which are for getting things done).

Well, kind of, not really: at its best prison bureaucracy is a heaving old machine that needs a virtuoso to get it working. When you can avoid it entirely, take the chance – for example, you can use 'wing reps' (prisoners on your wing who represent various bits of the jail) to send direct requests to the education, chaplaincy or health-care departments.

A lot of paperwork gets 'lost' – we call it the Bermuda Triangle of prison paperwork. Overworked prison officers simply haven't got the capacity to do more paperwork. For example, two months before my release my grandad died, but rather than process the paperwork required to let me out on an escorted visit to attend the funeral, they just – well – I don't know what they did, but I got no response whatsoever. On that note, if someone close to you dies while you're inside, you contact Cruse bereavement if you need help and support.

Even if your form avoids the bin, the complaints system is purpose designed to be impenetrable. I won't repeat what I said about the 'bitter cocktail', but it applies to this section too. And even if there was a complaint to make then a lot of prisoners have no faith at all in the system. I saw with my own eyes that this led to staff members taking the piss in full knowledge that nothing would ever be formalised against them.

So if you are a literate person banged up with all the time in the world then it's imperative that you stand up and fight The Battle of a Thousand Forms to prove they can't walk all over you, him, her and anyone else in the future, even if it sometimes does feel futile.

I could definitely draw comparisons between trying to escape prison's steel-clad concrete walls with a teaspoon and trying to get some results from the prison system by using the comps and apps on offer but I'd still encourage you to use it. Here's the technical process …

First, you write a Comp1 complaint form (receiving a useless response to this is just a formality). Then you write a Comp1a appeal form to take it up the management ladder. Write a Comp2 (light pink form) to 'confidentially' (I've included inverted commas because some prison officers will open them regardless) take it yet further. If you get another unsatisfactory response and you've got a valid point then write to the IMB (Independent Monitoring Board). Once you've gone through all the internal complaints process, write to the PPO (Prisons and Probations Ombudsman). You can also write to your MP, the Home Office, a solicitor who deals with jail issues or phone the ever-helpful PAS or Howard League advice line. It can take months to get a result but it's 100 per cent necessary. If the system gets told what's what and you've set a legal precedent, it will all seem worthwhile.

ELLIOT ON BEREAVEMENT

If you're unfortunate enough to suffer a loss while inside, it is possible to attend the funeral. From what I've seen this is normally only granted for members of immediate family, but is also dependent on risk factors such as your security category. My grandfather passed away while I was inside, after I'd been moved back to a Category C prison from a Category D prison following an unnecessary confiscation order which was imposed on me (long story short, they confiscated £300 and a battered old car – pointless).

Because my security category was still technically D, the lowest, I was allowed to be taken

to the funeral, but handcuffed to a prison officer. It wasn't a great experience, but I'm grateful I got to go.

Usually the chaplaincy or faith centre of the prison will handle such requests and ultimately, it's left to security to decide if you can be taken. You won't find out until the day of the funeral so as to avoid any potential advance escape planning. Either security will come to collect you or your religious representative will attempt to console you. Overall, a terrible experience, so ask your family to try and stick around on this mortal plane for a bit longer, at least until you get to Category D.

CODES OF CONDUCT

Prison is packed with manipulative and pugnacious people. And then there are the prisoners: most of them are a lot more harmless than the movies make out. Still, I'd recommend you keep yourself to yourself at first, work out who you can be yourself with, and eventually you'll make some life-long friends.

As soon as you walk on the wing you'll feel the eyes looking down at you, trying to assess where you slot into the hierarchy. It's a bit like when a new contestant walks onto a reality TV show, except one hundred times more tense. For the first fortnight you need to look grumpy and solely emit grunts to people you don't know; I call it the Fortnight Grump'n'Grunt.

After the nerves settle, male prison can just become one endless building site tea break. Banter about *Match of the Day* and *EastEnders*, shit-talk and gossip about screws and other prisoners, and the occasional

heart to heart. It's a weird form of socialising, because to an extent you always have to pull the shutters down on your true personality. Assuming a persona before you've even rubbed the sleepy dust out your eyes permanently distorts you, but it's an important survival technique.

The whole thing in the movies where someone goes straight up to the biggest guy in the prison and offers him out is a load of tripe. Put it like this: if you can survive a provincial British town at 1a.m. on a Friday night, where 9-5ers want a fight if they don't get a shag and a kebab, then you should be OK in prison.

Don't be wet, but at the same time don't walk around like Buzz Lightyear, don't steal from people, don't borrow things you can't pay back. And never ever grass anyone up - it won't get you an easier ride and the traditional punishment is getting your ear chopped off. You can't shake off the reputation, nor can you grow back an ear, so don't bother.

If someone does try it on with you then it's prudent not to let yourself get stood on. If you don't put up a fight you'll get classed as a pushover and then you really will get pushed over. What gets you respect is being vertebrate: straight up, reliable, funny, and helpful. If you're not adept in the bloke zone, then helping others to write applications, court appeals and letters will get you a long way.

I'm not going to lie though, I saw bad shit: vulnerable people getting terrorised for kicks, the manipulation of people with learning difficulties, razor blades melted into toothbrushes, unconfirmed sex offenders getting boiling water mixed with sugar poured over their heads, 30–man postcode fights and the occasional bit of 'claret' splattered up the wall. Most violence is to do with drugs and gang stuff so if you're not stepping on someone's toes either through dealing or debts then you should be alright.

However 'bad' someone thinks they are, no one really wants conflict at all. It's just an exacerbation of the negative male cultural standard. A lot of it is the same shit you see at school, down the pub, or in international politics: jail is an unrefined blokey zone with no mitigation. At least world leaders get to go to the golf club and whack golf balls. For prisoners there is no escape from the vicious cycle ... sadness, frustration, trauma, twistedness, people missing family and having not much to strive for. The atmosphere feels so brittle and explosive a lot of the time, and in my opinion it's surprising that even more violence and rioting doesn't happen. The only explanation I can give is that most prisoners are from backgrounds where they're already desensitised to it all.

Most violence happens behind cell doors, but when something is seen by officers you'll hear their radios make a noise like a siren and they will all run along to attend. If it's serious enough the jail will get put on 'lock down' which is just as it sounds: everyone is locked in their cell, the library, the classroom (or wherever else they may be) and no one can go on 'moves'.

When officers and prisoners scramble to see what's going on the 'peter thieves' will take their chance to do a bit of 'cell dipping'. I never had one thing stolen (by prisoners, that is) but I was still slightly cautious until I knew people on the wing.

I'd recommend you put your stuff away at 'sosh' (association time) because even if people don't try to steal something, if they spot it they'll end up looking round your door and doing your head, in asking if they can borrow it 24/7. Once you know your next–door neighbours they'll look out for you, but don't get too complacent. And don't get too complacent if you're a thief either: the traditional punishment for this is getting your fingers slammed in the door.

Now the nicer bit. You can and will make some really close mates – I'm still in contact with multiple people I met inside. Going through that whole experience together gives you a solidarity that is rare for our generation, and when we talk it feels like some kind of veterans' reunion.

The problem is that when you're playing coldhearted, your best mate could be two cells down from you, but you might end up never talking to them because you're both playing it cool, or should I say defensive and distrustful, so you never actually become friends.

Socialising is like a muscle and prison is like breaking your leg: once you get the cast removed, the muscle is atrophied and you can barely walk. I know from my own experience that it can take years to become healthy and open again – for this reason, making friends with other prisoners is crucial. One way to meet like-minded people is to work in a place like the gym, the library or as a Toe By Toe teacher. Or if you like a particular newspaper you can ask the newspaper orderly who orders similar publications to you (my mate calls this technique 'Guardian Cell Mates').

*

What else is there to mention? Asking people what they're in for is frowned upon – I'd avoid personal questions and let other people discuss what they're comfortable with. Also some people totally reinvent themselves in jail: I remember one guy scrounging noodles and I was thinking to myself, hang on, weren't you just telling everyone you're the Tony Montana of Tunbridge Wells and you've got a gullwing Lamborghini? Don't believe anything until you've triple checked, and this goes for what you hear from prisoners and screws alike.

JULIA ON THE FEMALE PRISON DYNAMIC

Once you have got over the initial shock and horror of the first week and you realise that prison is your new home for the foreseeable, it's important not to fight it, and to try to somehow get your head round your life in that moment. Don't forget, you are still a woman stuck in a system that was designed for men – it is even stranger for us, I reckon. Try and remember, it's not a place for ladies, so finding it so alien is to be expected.

I wasted way too much time thinking and torturing myself about the past, and some decisions I was agonising about the future couldn't be made at that time. You will hear people say 'Get your head in your sentence' or 'Get your head in here not "on road"' and suddenly one day, you realise they are right.

As silly as it sounds, my first question when I landed in the prison was, 'Can I have tweezers?'. The fear of ending up with a mono-brow was scary!

HAIRDRESSERS

In fact, you can get your hair cut and dyed in the hair salon, though be careful as these are performed by prisoners doing their NVQs – but on the flip side, there are some really talented ladies. Advice: chose your hairdresser wisely, unless you want a bowl cut!

There was also a beauty salon; in one prison I was in, you could even get a spray tan. You have to put in an application for these services and money is deducted from your prison account. In addition to this, you can order basic make-up, toiletries off the weekly canteen sheet.

You can order named brand products, which are pretty expensive as they are cheaper on the outside. You can place an Avon order every few months. There are some limitations as you aren't allowed glass bottles of aerosols. So, don't worry, you can still feel like yourself and try and look a bit glam and smell a bit better, but jail has a certain smell to it, no matter what you do. I remember coming home and trying to scrub the smell of jail off me.

Going to prison opened my eyes completely to the world and to myself. 'Normal' people go to jail – but why? So many ladies had been victims of abuse themselves, which led to mental health issues, addiction and offending. I remember one lady telling me that her parents had injected her with heroin at 11 years old; I couldn't believe what I was hearing. Like me, so many women had been through bad relationships and domestic abuse had left them with very low self-esteem.

Committing crime out of misplaced loyalty and bad decisions was a common theme. Female offending can be a result of emotional misjudgement. Many women had inadvertently committed 'secondary offences' to their partner's crime. They were under the misconception that the man would hold his hands up and rescue them from this complete nightmare. In fact, a lot of these men had no loyalty and just allowed their partners to take the charge.

Mental health is a huge problem in the female estate, with high rates of self-harm and suicide. Until I entered prison, I had never seen self-harm on such a scale. Sixty-five per cent of female prisoners reported having mental health issues according to one study.

One girl had cut her arms, legs and full body so many times that only her face was left free from cuts and devastating scars. Looking at people's lives, their problems and then the prison regime, it is completely understandable. There is some support for mental health, but not enough and this rarely continues through to the outside, so is never addressed fully.

The one positive thing I did to address my own low-level mental health issues, was life-coaching. Before I went into prison, I didn't think I had any issues – clearly I did! Be accepting of help and don't be afraid to admit to yourself that you may have mental health issues. I feel better now I have accepted that, and can move on.

Forming friendships and making associations in prison is very different to the real world. The bonds are so strong that they feel they will never break, but they are capable of breaking in a heartbeat. You will be shocked at your own emotions and how you become a different and softer version of yourself. I am not a 'huggy' person, wasn't before jail and I am not now, but in prison I found myself hugging *everyone*, walking round cuddling women that I had known two minutes.

I was really in touch with my emotional side: I was able to hide it in the outside world but in prison, I was really stripped back and needed the support. You believe that in prison you will need to be tough and in some situations you do, but when it comes to friendships, you feel a genuine sense of love and care, to others and yourself.

Female prisoners create a family dynamic that is different from what has been described in the male establishment. Some of the older and longer-serving prisoners feel like parents, your peers feel like siblings and some of the younger girls feel like your children. I remember some of the longer-serving ladies making my bed for me – I don't get such treatment at home! Thinking about it now, I was well looked after. I'd also like to mention the organisations Women In Prison, Woman At Wish and Clean Break, who give great support.

RACE AND RELIGION

You'll be asked to state your religion and ethnicity during your preliminary assessment. Eighteen religions are currently recognised by the prison service. Christian, Humanist, Hindu, Zoroastrian and Rastafarianism are included.

You'll be able to attend the relevant religious place on the relevant religious days (even if you're in segregation). You'll also be allowed the relevant artefacts – rosary beads (glow-in-the-dark ones are available from canteen!), prayer mats, miswak sticks, matzos, rune stones, incense … There's no official issue ganja for the Rastas, but it's everywhere on the wing, so don't worry too much.

The chaplaincy is able to help with a lot more than just confessing your sins – they can lend radios to prisoners, help with Sentence Planning and also run courses. They

have a lot of sway with the prison management and worth keeping in mind when you're in need.

The most popular religions in prison are Christianity and Islam. I apologise for my blasphemy but I went to Church just for some time out of my cell and to see mates from different wings. They'd play the hymns over a Casio keyboard beat and we'd sit on the pew right at the back, listening to our mate freestyling rhymes about the screws.

Converting to Islam in jail is a very big thing – Islam's popularity in British prisons has more than doubled over the last decade or so. I've seen white Islamic Geordie boys with a little ginger beard ('Y'alreet, mate, salamale-kum?') talking to black Islamic Brummie boys with more convincing beards ('Aleikum–salam, yes, my brudda!').

Some take Islam really seriously, others learn five Arabic words, stop eating pork and that's that – the older born-and-raised Islamic guys are really not feeling that lot! However, they are better at Islam than I am at Christianity so I won't pass comment.

There are a lot of reasons for Islam's popularity behind bars: firstly, there's the spirituality and the beliefs ... religion can provide a strong set of rigid values in a place that is often lacking in them. Secondly, it's social – you get time at the mosque and you get unlocked more than other prisoners during Ramadan (the ninth month of the Muslim calendar). Third – and I'm paraphrasing my Muslim convert mates when I say this, so don't shoot the messenger – it gives people a unified front against a system that never gave them total acceptance. The more the system and the media hype up Islam as the anathema, the more appealing it becomes.

Of course I've got to mention radicalisation. If a white system makes it virtually impossible to stay on the straight and narrow then a white policeman, white judge and white prison officer create a situation where you and nearly all your mates are locked up, and then a self-styled Emir turbo charges it all. Really, you'd expect a lot more people to get radicalised than actually happens. The media love to talk about it, but it's a rarity.

All of which brings me on to race. Statistically, it's a fact that non-white people are disproportionately targeted by police, more likely to receive custodial sentences and then receive longer sentences than their direct white counterparts. Once in prison it's more of the same: you're more likely to get nicked for the same offence and be put in solitary if you're non-white. It is a racist system – that's not an opinion, those are the facts of the situation.

Understandably, ethnic minority prisoners in particular have no faith in the system so only a fraction of racial complaints get formalised, but if you do fancy it then fill out a DIRF (Discrimination Incident Report Form) and contact the Equality And Human Rights Commission. You might also be able to talk to a Prison Equality Representative although they don't exist in some jails – it used to be mandatory to have a Race Equality and Action Team Officer but this was changed in 2010.

All that said, British jail is not an American movie. Racial gangs exist, but it's not like you'll be forced to stab someone with a different skin tone. Prisoners who can't speak good English congregate together but that's just a practical thing. In my experience of London jails you'll see a dreadlock yardie who is mates with the Belfast beefcake, Hamid the Bengali is mates with Simon from Canning Town, David the Orthodox Jew pensioner used to give me matzos and I'd swap them with an Albanian bloke for cell-made yoghurt.

Related to all this is the issue of Immigration Detention Centres. They are pretty much the same as jail, except people are put in them for the crime of not having the correct passport. Everyone should watch the *Panorama* documentary about these places and read more on www. detainedvoices.com. Someone needs to write *Immigration Removal Centre – A Survival Guide*!

PART TWO: TAKING CARE OF YOURSELF

KEEPING IN TOUCH

Let me quote the government – 'close ties between prisoners and key family members can significantly reduce the risk of reoffending – which costs society £15,000,000,000 every year'. It's odd, then, that they charge prisoners nearly 20p a minute to call a mobile, they only give them two letters a week, they punish them by reducing their family visiting hours and they are currently on a campaign to shut inner-city prisons that are close to communities and relocate prisoners a million miles from nowhere.

The phone

You'll find a couple of payphones (aka blue boxes) on every wing. They are eight times more expensive than an outside world payphone, which is terrible but still an improvement because up until 2016, they were 18 times more expensive. BT (the service provider) should be ashamed – if they are your service provider then cancel your contract and put your reasons on social media!

First, your numbers have to be pre-approved using a PIN Phone Application form. Once it's approved (and that can take a number of weeks, so I hope you're not in a rush), you'll be good to go. Then enter your eight-digit PIN security code (I entered it so many times I still type it on my phone if I'm half-awake, trying to call someone) – be careful with this code because if someone knows it, they can add their own numbers to your account and use your credit. Then enter the phone number. It'll start to ring – except it doesn't ring – it goes BEEP *your call is being connected* BEEP *your call is being connected*. Be careful not to connect to an answerphone because this will still suck your credit – I counted the exact number of beeps it took and made sure to hang up at the right moment to save precious pennies.

There's often a queue of people waiting to call, so it's not ideal if you're feeling really emotional. And you're limited to ten minutes per call.

In modern times we expect people to be connected constantly so if someone doesn't answer the phone you can feel seriously paranoid – you're like, *oh no, they don't love me any more* when really they just left their phone on silent. And vice versa – if you've arranged to talk at a specific time and the prisoner doesn't call then you can be like, *oh no, have they been hospitalised or put in segregation*? but no, it just turns out that they weren't unlocked because of staff shortages.

Different sides of the wall are a tale of two realities so you shouldn't expect your friends on the outside to orientate their entire existence around you. Trying to keep your relationship as a healthy proportion of your life is nigh on impossible; nothing to do, feeling mega sad, you start to feel needy even if you're usually a vision of independence.

Don't forget that everything – except legal calls – is monitored so don't say something silly like 'Call me back on my mobile' if you've got one. Which brings me on to mobiles. First things first, having a mobile phone in prison is highly illegal.

The prison service and the media always say that people have phones to control major drug gangs or whatever. I mean, I'm sure a couple do, but the truth is that most people simply have phones so they can stay in contact with friends and family, chat privately, use the internet, have a laugh.

The situation with phones has changed a lot in recent years. Prisons used to be a lot more hot on it, so it would be about sneaky avoidance techniques: looking out for phone scanners by keeping your TV on (if it flickers, they're using a signal detector), watching the shadows outside your cell, not using your phone during lunchtime bang up and being ready to jam it in your Chatham Pouch … I used to laugh at my mate boasting how he could plug an iPhone in a matter of seconds, made my eyes water at the thought. Nowadays you'll see staff just walking past prisoners scrolling through social media, both sides beyond caring.

There are a couple of private businesses that offer good services if you're trying to keep it straight and narrow. The first is PrisonPhone.co.uk, who offer savings of up to 75 per cent: the prisoner calls a landline number, which is much cheaper, and then the call is forwarded to your mobile; if you do the maths, it could save you a lot of money. Another service is PrisonVoicemail.com, a service you have to pay for monthly. You leave a voice message for your loved one, they then call up a landline to listen and record a response for you. They also have an app to notify them that they have a message. I haven't used it, but I've heard it's a good service – check their website for details.

Letters

Letters are a serious lifeline. You might feel like you're in a period drama sitting down with pen and paper, I hadn't written since school so I was totally out of practice, my arm moved like a drunken bloke trying to dance salsa. You'll soon realise though that sitting at that desk gives you time to articulate complex stuff in a way that you just can't with rushed phone calls and pressurised visits. It's the nearest you'll get to genuine interaction with the people you're closest to, which, as I've already said, is what you'll probably miss the most.

People will feel pressure to write deep and meaningful odysseys. Those letters are great but I valued equally mindless scribbles that more resembled text messages just to keep me in the social loop. So, if you're sending mail to someone inside, keep the scribbles and gossip flowing, print articles for them, take screenshots and print them at Boots using one of those photo-printing kiosk machines. Even if you're having an alright time in prison, you feel unbelievably trapped while the outside world keeps moving – it can feel like you've been cryogenically frozen.

If you're supporting someone inside: keep stamps in your wallet, throw whatever it is straight into the postbox, it doesn't have to be a detour or a hassle. You must include their prisoner number and your full name and return address (although they have no way of checking that those details are legit). Correspondence is not allowed to be 'offensive' and can't name victims or compromise the security of the prison – all this should be patently obvious. Letters can also be sent using www.emailaprisoner.com for less than the price of a stamp – it's simple, quick and cheap. To contact the contributors of this book who are still in jail, I relied upon this service: it's great. From some jails the prisoner can respond digitally (they can scan the letter) but in others you still have to respond by post. While in a Category B prison, I received a fiver in a letter – not that it had any value at all on the wing but I showed it to someone doing life and they were like 'what the …!' They hadn't seen money for about 20 years.

The wing office should give you two postage-paid envelopes a week. A lot of people don't use theirs so it's worth asking around if you need more. And, again, don't forget that the mail is monitored, especially if you're on 'monitored mail' (wing staff will be able to tell you if you are). The prison is not allowed to monitor your legal letters, though. You can seal these and write RULE39 on them and they're supposed to be left unopened although prisons have been found to abuse this rule. Don't think you can just write to your mate about escape plans and stick RULE39 on the front and they won't notice, though, as they compare the name and address to a list of solicitors and courts.

If people don't end up writing back to you then you shouldn't get too offended. Before I went to prison one of my ex-prisoner friends told me, 'You will find out who your fake friends are because they won't write you' ... then he never wrote to me! I didn't think he was fake though, I just figured he was busy – life on The Out is hectic – he's still my friend to this day.

Maybe at a party get everyone to sign something and post it off – believe me, receiving something like this in your cell makes you feel so wicked.

Penpal services that support prisoners are brilliant. If you are a prisoner who gets no letters then you can give your address to www.prisonerspenfriends.org. If you're LGBTQ+, then write to the excellent Bent Bars Project (page 202).

If you want to write to prisoners yourself, as some-one on the outside, then it's worth touching on the tone of these kinds of letters: if I was receiving one of them, then I'd like more positive connection and interesting stories than 'poor old you' or 'what did you do?' because I'm a complete human, not just a committer of a crime. Just be sensitive until you know each other a bit better and always be confidential if you want open and honest chat – a lot of prisoners are scared of being open for a raft of reasons! And don't get involved unless you're serious about writing – if you write only one letter then don't bother with another it can be so wounding for a prisoner. I feel like the people who most need this kind of service often don't know it exists so if you are on the wing, then spread the word.

Other bits you can send in

Books. Until very recently there used to be a lot more freedom to send books to prisoners but then the Right Honourable Chris Grayling MP banned the sending of books for 'security reasons'. Currently, you can order them brand new from a small range of online retailers (sendbookstoprisoners.co.uk offers a free service that explains every prison's particular requirements for sending in books). The new system sucks: a limited range of titles from certain online retailers. The cherry on the cake is that the last time I sent a book to Sarah Jane Baker, I followed all rules exactly and it was still rejected for no apparent reason.

Cards. You can't send in musical cards, glitter, or anything padded. Have a go at making stuff DIY rather than buying something from the high street – it'll most likely stay on the prisoner's wall until they're released!

Pictures. You can't send photos of the following: explicit stuff, the prisoner themselves (in case they try to bodge some kind of ID card) or pictures of children unless they are family (enclose an explanatory note if this is the case).

Clothes. To pass clothes out, use 'hand out apps'. To bring clothes in, the prisoner probably needs to fill in forms to get them approved – check the C.R.A.P. beforehand.

VISITS

Visits are a strange airlock between prison and the real world. A visit is definitely nothing like an ordinary interaction.

In the run-up to the visit the way some boys prepare is like they're going on *X Factor*. Fresh haircut, pluck their monobrow, iron their shirts. Then just before the visit, while you're held in a little holding cell, those boys are doing push-ups so the blood is flowing to their pecs and biceps and they are the buffest they can possibly be.

You'll be watched over by CCTV cameras and over-zealous screws. All the prisoners are sat there wearing hi-vis tabards like kids on a school outing, trying not to spill the emotional beans, almost overdosing on sweets and fizzy drinks you rarely get on the wing. Partners' eyes are fake eye-lashed and eye-shadowed up to the max, parents' eyes are looking baggy after years of this shit, children's eyes are wide open wondering why Daddy can't leave the school he goes to. Everyone's constantly looking out the corner of their eye at the clock counting towards kick-out time, either itchy to leave or desperate to stay forever.

If it's a visit with your partner then I think for both sides, walking in and seeing that person is like going on a first date even though you might have known each other for years. You feel shy and confused. Touching legs, hugging and kissing, and sorry to be crude but tracksuits and semis don't go well together. People want more than just their forearm stroked, obviously, and as the screws turn their backs there's a Mexican wave of grope, everyone trying for a glimmer of physicality.

Even if it's just with your mates then being in that room after stewing in the same-sex cesspit of the wing, the visit room is like carnal technicolor. Don't sit there staring at someone else's girlfriend. Fights kick off over this stuff and it's good for no one. Have respect.

In real life people rarely talk to each other solidly for two hours, but in a visit you're sat directly opposite each other and you feel awkward if you can't keep the conversation going constantly from start to finish. If you do cut the visit short, the screws tend to strip-search you on the assumption that the visit was just a business transaction. It's also worth mentioning that lip readers and directional microphones are used so if you're on remand for something serious, don't talk about your case or cover your mouth and whisper when you do.

Passing contraband is so common that you'll see it out the corner of your eye at least once or twice. There are loads of techniques, pretty much all of them very well known to the screws. Don't think you're original spitting drugs into a Coke can, that one's as old as the hills. Passing drugs is a gamble that goes right most of the time but if it doesn't, family or friends might just get a sentence of their own. Being pushed to bring in drugs is a big thing, but if you're a visitor and you're asked to do this, just politely say no if that's an option. I remember in Wormwood Scrubs there was a whiteboard that said NUMBER OF VISITORS ARRESTED and underneath was a number that went up a chunk after every visit. Also, if you get caught, you can get put on Closed Visits.

I remember my friend told me he tried to book a visit for three consecutive days, but there was no answer and no answerphone – the phone just rang and rang and rang. On the fourth day the phone was picked up, a voice shouted, 'PICK UP THE DAMN PHONE,' then promptly hung up. Thankfully, the useless old system of visiting orders has been replaced by the MoJ online booking service. The prisoner will have to add the visitor to their online list, then they'll be able to book visits quite easily.

If you're visiting someone, you can get help with costs from the Assisted Prison Visits Unit if you are on benefits or have a low income and you are close family or their sole visitor. You can only get assistance for two visits per month, they rarely assist with accommodation however far away from home the prison is, often they take ages to pay and don't answer the phone for months at a time – being punished just for being poor once again. I've included the APVU phone number in the Useful Contacts section although I'm not sure that they belong there.

I'll tell you some additional information, but bear in mind this might be C.R.A.P. because different jails operate differently: you can normally have up to three people visiting you at any one time, convicted prisoners get between one and four visits per month, remand prisoners can get three visits a week, some jails have really good family visits, you can double up visits if the prison is a long way from home – once again, you should check the *Inside Time* website for concise and up-to-date visiting information for your particular prison.

I should also quickly mention official visits: there are legal visits (your solicitor will know the deal on these) for which you can get a one-hour visit in a private room for confidentiality, or it can be done by videolink. There are also police visits if they're investigating something – you can't be forced to turn up but if a judge comes, then it's a crime not to attend, and that's a separate offence.

If you get a no-show it's horrible being left, sat in the visit room feeling like a lemon. A handful of people get turned away from visits because they haven't dotted their Is or crossed their Ts, or because they have forgotten their ID, so make sure you have everything straight.

When I visited a friend recently a fingerprint system had been introduced. The idea is that on your first visit you provide ID and scan your prints, then on following visits you'd only need to bring your fingers. Which is good, because forgetting your fingers is difficult. Except they also said to still always bring your ID just in case the system fails.

TRYING TO STAY SANE

OK, this section is where it gets real, where I go into the way a human brain responds to a place like prison. If you have a weak constitution then I suggest you skip the next few pages.

Mental health awareness is a serious thing nowadays. Everyone from heavyweight boxers to investment bankers is Instagramming about their depression and anxiety. Maybe one day this mental health renaissance will be extended to the lowest echelons of society.

Your mind is as sparse as the cell you're locked in. The tinny tinkle from the officers' keys echoes around your cell in the same way that the most minor thought can rattle round your head. Torturous over-thinking of a meaningless statement, a past trauma, or a small conflict with someone on the wing can lead to spiralling neurosis you wouldn't be a part of if you were in the outside world or simply had something to distract you.

That place will push you as low as you can go so if you're someone who can go low, expect to go lower. The depression can be contagious. Hard-as-nails geezers respond by taking it out on others, self-harmers cut up their arms, drug users are expected to stay clean, but who knows how they're meant to, and previously OK people turn to all of the above because very little else is on offer. To stay afloat, you need a Teflon mindset.

I have the potential to be a very depressive person but stay just about alright by keeping overwhelmingly busy. In jail some people might call me a fraggle (a weak-minded person) for saying that, but I think most prisoners would tell you the same if they were being honest. Once that door locks and the banter stops, your thoughts can do weird things. I just sat there feeling hazy blue, wanting either a deep and emotional conversation with someone I loved, or some privacy and silence, getting angry and frustrated because I knew all of those were a long way away.

I think the best compromise can be writing everything out on paper even if you just throw it away. It can help you organise your thoughts so they seem slightly more logical. Dismantling the machine and seeing the components helps you understand what's going on, if you know what I mean.

You feel real laziness too: people say 'Sleep away your bird' because they'd prefer to be in the Land of Nod than that shithole cell. You have nowhere to go except bed and all that sleep makes you feel even sleepier and shittier, back hurting from lying down too much. Your brain feels a mess and your feet are all cheesy but you can't even be bothered to drag yourself to the kettle on the other side of the cell, let alone the shower.

You'll be lucky if there's someone you can tell how you really feel, or you might be so worried they'll ask how you are when you don't even want to be confronted by that question, so you don't even ring them if they're there for you. And even if you did want to talk about it all, you don't have time enough on the phone and there's a queue of blokes telling you to hurry the fuck up because they want to talk to their kids too. Hmm.

If you're on the outside and you are worrying about a prisoner then you can contact the Safer Custody Team. Every jail has one: some have emails, some have phone numbers; they normally only respond during working hours. And if there is an emergency – for example, a death or serious illness in the family – you need to inform the prisoner immediately. You should telephone the main prison number and explain the problem to the operator, who will transfer you to the appropriate person.

For a lot of prisoners their way out is self-harm. You'll walk around and see forearms so cut up with razor scars that the skin looks like a thatched roof. There are many different reasons for this: they shouldn't be lumped together or judged. If you feel like 'cutting up', you'd probably like a time machine to relive certain bits of your life, or a lot of therapy and love, which is definitely not available behind bars. All I can do in these circumstances is tell you the meagre services available. Ring the cell buzzer (which can take hours to be answered – sometimes they ring all night) and tell a member of staff: they are trained to cope with crisis-stricken prisoners. However, if I was feeling like that personally, I'd prefer to deal with another prisoner, like a Listener.

A Listener is a prisoner accredited by the Samaritans to support their peers. In most jails they wear green t–shirts or orange fleeces and have notices on the out-side of their cells denoting where you can find them when needed. If need be, even while you're banged up staff can let them come to your cell and talk things through. You can also phone the Samaritans free from the wing payphone. However, again, crying your eyes out and talking about suicidal thoughts on the wing is highly impossible for reasons I mentioned before. You can also write to them (address at the back of this book, page 202) but it takes a while for a response, so you might not hear back when you most need it.

To become a Listener you'll have to have a while left to serve, have a clean record and be on enhanced. It's quite obviously a good thing to do while you're in jail in order to help others but also for yourself and your *self*. You get trained to give others the skills to articulate and under-stand their own emotions and this will in turn help you to rationalise your own feelings to yourself. It's a really good way to get involved, one of the few ways to get that rewarding feeling of communal contribution in prison.

There's another reason why people self-harm in prison. Some just do it because it is the only way they can get attention from overstretched authorities. The understaffed and overpopulated system often totally ignores requests both big and small (from answers about parole board hear-ings, wanting to get moved to a prison closer to friends and family, attending a funeral or just getting a dental appointment to fix a toothache) but when prisoners self-harm, a report must get written by officers. Prisoners who cut up are put on ACCT (Assessment Care in Custody and Teamwork) and the SCT (Safer Custody Team) will be obliged to listen to your concerns.

Mental health services have been cut back to the extent that if you simply request to get seen then you may not be seen for forever and a day, however self-harming will get you onto the hospital wing immediately. I would never ever recommend taking this course of action but this is simply the current state of prisons ... putting a razor in your arm is the only tool available to many people trapped in the system.

And – obviously – it gets worse. A massive proportion of prisoners have pre-existing mental health issues and that dirty white little cell amplifies the worst thoughts. Anxieties, traumas and schizophrenic tendencies combine with the stresses of prison and result in a shockingly high number of people hanging from light fixings. The system isn't doing nearly enough to prevent this. In fact 70 per cent of people who died from self-inflicted means while in prison had already been identified as having mental health needs and nearly one in five of those diagnosed with a mental health problem received no care from a mental health professional while in prison.

When it comes to an issue such as this, a book by a stranger can offer platitudes at best.

The only really constructive advice I have is for the Ministry of Justice but they've heard the same stuff a million times from a million people and the rates of self-harm and suicide keep rising at a horrific rate. This is the human cost of running a cheap-as-chips lock'em-up-system.

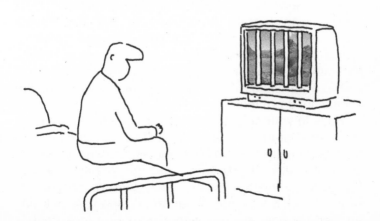

Escapism did me a lot of good. With a big metal door and bars on the window, and a lack of armed gunmen, helicopters and angle grinders, the only place you can escape to is inside your head. Television is the escapism of choice and becomes a surrogate family for a majority of prisoners. After your door is locked at 5pm it's straight *Neighbours – Simpsons – EastEnders – Corrie – Enders* part two channel ping-pong until lights out. I always found it funny that free people watch endless prison dramas like *Orange Is the New Black*, and prisoners watch endless freedom dramas like *EastEnders*.

I watched a lot of TV but I felt like books offered me so much more potential for escapism. I had hardly read since I left school but by the time I was released, I'd eaten through almost every classic on the bookshelf. I came out feeling sharper than ever.

KEEPING FIT

With the crap food and sedentary lifestyle it requires a lot of self-discipline to avoid becoming a bunk bed potato. However, body image is one of the only things to really focus on so you'll see prisoners who look like Michelangelo's David except dressed in a trackie.

The gym's smell is unbearable but the atmosphere is unreal ... vests, clanking iron and tunes ... Polish meatchunks who speak Jamaican slang helping Vietnamese Mancunians do their bench press. Even if you've never lifted a finger nail to scratch your head, you should get down there.

Back in your cell you should get on a fitness regime: press-ups, sit-ups, squats, turn a chair upside down and do dips, benchpress the bunk bed, lift the biggest bottles you can find, do headstand press-ups against the wall. I used to do this stuff every tenth page of my book or advert break on TV until I ran around the yard one day and felt my pecs bounce with every step I took; feeling

like I had breast implants was too weird so I cut down on it. There's a book called *Cell Workout* by ex-prisoner L.J. Flanders that really goes in on this stuff if you want to know more.

HEALTH

Prison and physical health are not partners in crime. To see a medical professional (dentist, nurse, doctor), you'll need to put in an application. If you're prescribed med- icine, you'll need to collect it twice a day from the meds hatch on the 1s. Some people will need the standard antibiotics, insulin, arthritic anti-inflammatory pills, but the large majority of the meds queue is drug users getting their methadone. It's hectic and there are various jokes about the queue, but I won't repeat them here. You'll need your prisoner ID card to collect meds and when you swallow pills, you'll need to prove you've washed them down – there's a massive black market for prescription drugs.

Disabilities include the obvious things like being in a wheelchair or having learning difficulties but also include diabetes, clinical depression, deafness and anything else that changes the way you live your life. You shouldn't be discriminated against but it's hard not to see the prison system itself as discriminatory – severe depressives are locked up 23 hours a day and type 1 diabetics (like myself) eat the tiny portions of crap food and get virtually no exercise to burn it off. Every time I go to the diabetes centre at my local hospital, the government tells me to eat healthily, test regularly and do a lot of exercise ... but when that same government sent me to prison they stuck me in a box, fed me absolute shite and often didn't let me test sugars or do insulin between 5pm bang up and 8am unlock the next morning. I was recently told by a MoJ healthcare provider that you're allowed to keep your testing kit in your cell, but this was never the case for me despite my NHS diabetes consultant and myself writing endlessly to the Governor.

The situation for deaf people is bad in a way that's often not considered – while you might not categorise having banter as a human right, in prison it becomes something you completely rely on because your other senses are so under-stimulated.

In my opinion, if you've got learning difficulties then you simply shouldn't be in prison. I saw people who were not able to cope with the experience being wound up, bullied and fed drugs just for jokes. The amount of people in prison with major and minor mental disabilities would be a scandal in a civilised country and – again – I have no advice for you, but I've got a lot for the Ministry of Justice.

The prison should make adaptations to care for you. In my own experience as a diabetic I was given a 'diabetes pack' at dinner every night. It contained a piece of fruit and a mini-carton of UHT milk. If you feel that the prison should make adjustments to better care for you then apply to see the Disability Liaison Officer. I've only discovered their existence since researching this book – these things are kept under wraps when you're on the wing.

Untold amount of fights happen just because of toothache. You have to put in a healthcare app and wait. And wait. And wait.

If you have a serious health problem you'll be taken to an outside hospital. Escapes happen this way so expect to be handcuffed to an officer and expect it to take a while. Someone I know got his arm broken and then waited three whole days before he was seen to, and I'm sure there are worse horror stories.

Most charities specialising in a particular disability or disease will offer some information about coping with that condition in prison although in my experience their advice is often very unrealistic: they talk about it from the book (the government's book, not mine) rather than from any type of experience. Basically, if a charity says something like 'it is challenging' then you should already know that this is a euphemism for 'it is a total nightmare'.

Healthcare workers (some are NHS, but many are agency workers with very little job security) occupy an odd zone because they're neither prisoners nor prison officers. People latch onto them and want to chat because they're like a message in a bottle from the outside world. Some of them are up for the chat, but others are sick to death of being shouted at for methadone and nicotine patches or just in a rush to get each prisoner processed in ten seconds flat.

To complain about treatment of a disability then go through the usual avenues for complaint. You can also speak to or write to PAS. To complain about the NHS healthcare provision, check the PAS Healthcare Complaints sheet that is specifically about this process.

SEX

Prison exacerbates the worst bits of male behaviour (more anger, more fighting, fewer emotional outlets, less sensitivity) – and massively reduces the more positive aspects of masculinity (for example being a good father and good partner).

Sex is obviously a key part of positive loving relationships. Many countries see conjugal visits as a right and an important element in maintaining prisoners' relationships and therefore their rehabilitation. However, there are no conjugal visits in British prisons. So it doesn't matter if you're the Sexy Felon or a bag of spuds, you're most likely going to have a dry patch while behind bars. Besides making a hole in your mattress, it's just you and your grubby mitts.

Phone sex with a bunch of blokes queuing behind you and staff monitoring the call might not appeal, but you might overhear other prisoners having a good time with it. Sex writing too – don't know, not my scene, but have a crack.

Long story cut short: consensual heterosexual physical relationships are not happening unless it's with a staff member (much rumoured, but not very common) or tantric mindsex with your girlfriend in the visit room (not much rumoured and really not common ... maybe look up Casey Hardison for advice about this if you're interested).

Most female officers are completely professional but some absolutely thrive on the sexual attention from all the pent-up and pumped-up muscular bad boys. They come in the cell, sit on the bed and wind you up to near popping point. It all sounds like a laugh but in reality it can be a strange, unhealthy and mutually abusive dynamic – many officers who start to feel amorous towards a prisoner wind up being manipulated to smuggle in phones and drugs, and sometimes end up in prison themselves. I saw this happen with my own eyes.

Talking of staff, I did feel pretty sorry for the ones who have to do the mid-evening check, where they walk round after everyone's been locked up and and open the door observation flaps to check nothing's gone awry. I imagine it's like Chat Roulette – that website where you can videochat with random people across the world, where two-thirds of people want to have a nice chat with a stranger and a third is just men masturbating ...
opens flap oh, he's writing a letter
opens flap oh no, he's crying into his pillow
opens flap oh, he's having a wank

If you're anything like me then your desire will just pla-teau or wither. With no porn, no conjugal visits and no new deposits in the old 'wank bank', it all gets a bit bland – you'll probably be halfway through and end up thinking of something more important like 'Maybe I can blag the education department for a new pen tomorrow'.

Don't Drop the Soap is a laddish thing to say when someone is going to prison – it basically means 'You're going to get raped'. You'd think prison rape was every-where and unavoidable the amount it gets bandied about. I don't mean to downplay it, it does happen, but I literally never saw or heard about it.

However, maybe this is because people feel unable to report or openly discuss sexual assault. If you are harassed or sexually assaulted, it's probably the worst place to experience such a thing. I'd suggest you talk to a Listener or a member of staff and they will hopefully take the issue very seriously. Sexual assault is a crime behind bars as much as it is in the outside world. But prisons are known to cover up the issue and be reluctant to call in the police – if this is the case then you should kick up a fuss until you're heard, although kicking up a fuss is most likely the last thing you want to do.

JULIA ON BEING 'GAY FOR THE STAY'

Same-sex relationships are completely the norm in female establishments – it's so different to male prison in this respect. In my experience, homophobia in female jails is very rare – in fact, getting a bird while doing your bird is more than encouraged!

I am straight (ish!) but I had two relationships while in prison. I am completely at ease with my sexuality and don't really like labels, but going into prison is like a whole different world. Don't worry, you don't get pounced on, but it's likely you may receive some attention. Some of the girls actually look like really attractive boys, and you have to take a second look!

A lot of ladies form relationships with other females that would be so unlikely in the cultural environment of the everyday outside world.

Some girls had their fellas on the out, then their girls on the inside. It was comical seeing girls on visits with their men, then their bird was sat on the other side of the visiting hall. It did cause some people a great of conflict, as it was hard for them to see past the daily reality and deal with their outside lives. They ultimately did this when they left, leaving one upset girl in prison. Although, the upset girl often moved on very quickly to the next one!

For me, having these relationships was more of a comfort and without my second 'bird', I really wouldn't have got through my sentence. She was my protector and my comfort.

Now down to the nitty-gritty ... sex in prison! Having sex with someone for the first time in real life is scary enough, but having sex with someone for the first time in prison is off the scale. First, you are stone-cold sober, you have to navigate through roll check and screws casually wandering in, plus it's with a woman and really, I had no clue what I was doing. Looking back, I was probably a right disappointment and would have been literally shaking in fear. It's funny thinking about it now – not so much at the time.

I was released before her, and she had another year or so to go. When I was in jail, I actually believed that I could be with her in real life but as soon as I walked through those gates, I knew that it wasn't the real me and I wasn't gay ... or should I say, I was just 'gay for the stay!'

You are allowed to get married or enter into a civil partnership while in prison. It's quite a complicated process but this shouldn't stop you if you're in true love, sat in a cell with nothing else to do. Section 14/2016 of the Prisons Service Instructions gives the full lowdown but the basics are that if you have more than three months left to serve, you'll most likely be granted permission;

if you're a lower category prisoner, you'll most likely be able to have it outside (with prison officers watching) and if you're higher category, it'll be held in the jail's chapel. Friends and family will be able to attend but they'll probably have to buy the Bible from an authorised retailer. And your honeymoon won't be in Barbados on a deckchair, it will be in the visit room on a plastic chair bolted to the floor.

HAVING A PARTNER IN PRISON

LISA SELBY ON HAVING A PARTNER IN PRISON

Often, when you tell people that your loved one is in prison, you're met with shock, surprise or fear. Unfortunately, many people still hold ill-informed prejudices and will be unsympathetic towards your situation. The first question they'll want to throw at you will be the nature of the offence, as it's a natural curiosity. You're under no obligation to disclose the offence, let alone offer a justification for it. So be prepared for the input of the uninformed, as everybody turns into an armchair solicitor when it comes to discussing crime and prison. This does, however, make it so much more refreshing when you do actually meet someone who is educated about the subject, or at least open-minded enough to take into account the opinions of others. Some may try to hide the fact a loved one is in prison out of shame and stigma, by saying they are travelling or working away. It's important to educate those

who are on the outside because they are the people your loved one will be either embraced or rejected by when they are released. Let's face it, they've had enough isolation and rejection imposed upon them by the system already, we don't need to make it worse.

PRISON WIVES

We call ourselves Prison Wives, even if we're not married by law. We play the supporting role and get no glory and no understanding: we're like the footballer who provides the crucial pass for the striker to score a goal – we feel left behind when the cameras only zoom in on him. For the thousands of partners whose life is also dominated by the prison system, there is virtually no support in practical or financial terms.

I've been to prison despite never being arrested. I hear prison sounds in my ear when he phones, I can smell prison food when I visit, I can feel prison stigma from the community and that's only the tip of the iceberg. My mental health has been tested to the max, but these are the things we do for love. We instinctively know that our care can be the maker or breaker of the future of that person's entire freedom.

I should also quickly mention that it's thought that one in six prisoners receive no visits whatsoever. Also, many prisoners are in same-sex partnerships and can't even show the limited amount of affection I'm about to describe due to homophobia.

THE BEGINNING: MAKING THE DECISION TO STAY OR GO

Prison is like a washing machine for love – a lot of relationships will get washed down the drain, the ones that last will most likely fade and only a few will hold fast. It can be years of emotional, financial and sexual frustration and can literally be endless if someone's on an indefinite sentence. Many partners flop, cheat or look back wishing they'd left at the beginning – to fall apart on a prisoner while they are sitting in a cell is prolonged torture for them – the first thing you should do is to be frank: are you up for the struggle?

IF YOU GO

There will be guilt and I'm sure people will be judgemental – but I doubt they know how hard it really is. Maybe they'll understand your reasoning and if it's real then maybe you'll rekindle things once they are released. You may even want to continue to support and visit them as a friend.

IF YOU STAY

Prisoners often get arrested at a lifetime low; therefore relationships are often at their worst point too. Partners are often (not always) at the tail end of a wave of self-destructiveness and selfishness: lies, secrecy and crimes behind your back. Maybe you've been sat at home, out of your mind, wondering where they are, wondering why money, drugs or lifestyle are more important than you and your love. Often, they go to prison and you're left on the outside, cleaning up the emotional and financial chaos they've left behind ... but now they're in prison they're all sorry and need all your help. It can be hard to provide, to say the least.

They are a part of you and now they are part of the system. Love is a heart-shaped peg and imprisonment is a cell-shaped hole (lined with barbed wire). You are not evolved or educated to reconcile these two things.

Some people spend their time waiting, cherishing the last moments they were together. Playing them over and over in their head, as if they had broken up or even as though their partner has passed away. In a functional, 'normal' sense they are no longer there, so I suppose it's understandable. Prison Wives often have their partner as their screensaver and will download a countdown app on their phone that tells them how many days left and shows a pie chart of served vs. time to go. You'll be his 'Google Nurse' looking up everything from football scores to indigestion remedies made from the ingredients available on the canteen – to the extent that targeted advertising on my social media isn't sure if I'm a teacher or an imprisoned ex-drug user.

LOVE, AKA ...

Obsession? Prison love can look a lot like it. If you're not there exactly when he needs you, it can feel as though you're being dismissive.

You're on his wall, in his every single thought. Your number will be the top on his phone list, you're his confidante.

Possession? Prison loves can look extremely dated. We present ourselves in a sexually over-stated way in the visit room, we shape our lives around our partners, we send them amorous postcards and on forums we even talk about them as 'Our Boys' – it can all feel very wartime.

Some Prison Wives actually prefer some aspects of their loved ones being inside, because of the intensity, and the focused atten-tion. Before he went to prison he might've been a total bastard, but now he's sending you hand-written love poems, he calls you first thing, and you know exactly where he is! But, are we all cruising for a failure with that relationship model? It wasn't like that before, so how will it be after?

VISITS

A prison visit is a glimpse into their world – the blokey zone full of grey tracksuits, tattoos and grumpy faces – and it's a lot like being in prison yourself even if you're only a visitor.

They often can be very far from home, so if you don't drive, expect a long journey using whatever public transport and taxis are on offer. It will consume time and money you simply may not have. By the time you arrive you'll be tired and running on pure nerves, excitement, anger or maybe all of them at once.

Nobody greets you and says, 'Are you OK? This is actually going to be quite daunting for you, you are going to be really shaken up by this.' There's no positive encouragement, just rules (I've put the entire visitors' rules list on prison-ism.co.uk). You'll probably learn them either by stepping out of line without realising or friendly advice from other visitors.

Some of the officers are great, but others are on a power trip that you can't challenge. A good interaction with the prison staff results in a better mood, results in good energy with your partner, results in them behaving level-headed once they're back on the wing – and vice versa. You get to know the good screws by name and it makes such a massive difference when they're on duty.

The newer visitors sometimes look like they're going out clubbing, all dressed up for a night out. The ladies are making sure they look their best and the toilets are thick with hairspray and perfume. The regulars will more often think of comfort, wearing trackies and trainers.

After you've provided the proper ID you'll sit in a waiting room, overhearing stilted conversations about 'So how long has he got left?' and 'Did you see her ... ? I can't believe they let her in, looking like a stripper ... I had every inch of me covered last week and they threatened to issue me with a ban ... '. You can only take in change, ID and the clothes you're wearing. The lockers are always broken and tiny – I have had

to stash my belongings in the bushes outside in the past.

Then you'll get called in. It's time for a search. You'll get weirdly used to the intrusive levels of it all. Step forward, open your mouth, raise your arms; they'll quickly pat you down, turn around and the same again. Children look very confused at first, but get used to it. Screws often joke to them about how they need to behave, as though they're at school.

Posters will warn you:

Please use the toilet facilities before entering the visits hall as you will not be able to use them whilst on your visit unless there are exceptional circumstances: Unless you have a medical condition (you need to bring evidence of this). Unless you need to change your baby's nappy. Unless your child needs to use the facilities (under 16s). Unless you are pregnant.

Warning: CCTV cameras are used in this area (even by the reception lockers).

No photos. No mobile phones. You will be fined up to £2,000 or go directly to prison if you disobey these rules.

Attention, stand here.

If you chose to leave the visits area, your visit will be terminated.

A kiss and embrace are allowed at the start and at the end of a visit only. This does not start when the five-minute warning is given. Holding hands is permitted as long as it is above the table and visible to staff at all times.

Let me describe the context. The visit room floor tends to be lined with speckled industrial hospital lino or contract carpet. The chairs are often locked to the floor to prevent them being used as weapons (which also means you can't sit close to one another). Everything comes in shades of light blue, peach, turquoise, depending on the prison – exactly like a hospital – multi-coloured but soulless.

So then you'll head in. It's a rush, awkward and wonky. It can be shocking seeing them in person – their skin becomes paler than usual as they're hardly exposed to the sun. Sunburn isn't a thing in prison.

VITAMIN D

Often you feel very few emotions after the rigmarole of getting there but pretty soon you'll go to buy sausage rolls, Quavers and sugary cans. One jail I visited served a sandwich called the Visit Room Special – it was just ham and margarine. If you go at the start of the visit, you'll spend 15 minutes of your precious visiting time waiting in the queue. It's such a strange world: I've even known families who create their own sign language for items while queuing at the cafe and signalling to their loved one across the room – for a Galaxy bar, maybe they'll point to the sky, tea and coffee are the standard 'T' and 'C' with your hand, Nourishment is the pulling of a ring pull followed by a flexing muscle pose.

We have to try and reconnect in these restricted situations. Imagine being interrupted by kick-out-time on a visit, or by the bleeps or by a 30-second-man (the automated voice warning at the end of a phone call). The screws shout at you to stop your embrace. They shout at you to stop your conversation. They stand over you.

If you're like me, you'll hate seeing prison officers more intimate with your loved one than you can be – touching their whole body through polythene gloves, 'bending them up', telling them to drop their pants – it's an odd form of jealousy! I've seen men in the visits hall with numerous women coming and going, even though you saw them cosying up with their wife and kids for the past year. If you're trying to make it work with your loved one, you'll pray they are not one of those players; if you're faithful and live your life according to his schedule and needs, surely he wouldn't stoop so low?

Once you're in your seat you can't leave. You're in prison – so if you see a fight kicking off or another woman having a rough emotional time, you will be ejected for trying to help. You can't pass her a tissue either as they're prohibited. If something kicks off then don't get involved, but try and be there afterwards for some supportive words and for some knowing looks.

If you're seen being too touchy-feely though you can have your visit terminated and he might get strip-searched. Also, you have to bear in mind family and kids are in the same room – it's an unimaginable cocktail of desire, decency and rules. I recently saw a woman cradling a baby detained for passing drugs.

Almost every other visit women are caught smuggling – mainly tobacco since it was banned. I once saw a woman get caught while cradling a baby; the prison called social services immediately. She seemed quite calm but we all had to watch, with the children and the newbie Prison Wives staring in shock.

I love connecting with those other women on a heartfelt level; sharing techniques about saving money, tips about the prison he wants to go to, even tattoos. Girls who are new to the system get overexcited and end up with hearts bursting through broken chains or script that says something like:*'You can lock the locks but can't stop the clocks'*.

Sometimes the journey home is the worst bit – the high is over and the comedown begins. You see people walking from a prison visit with their loved one out into a world where the newspapers tell everyone to lock them up and throw away the key. It's not an easy contradiction to cope with.

As systems change from one prison to another, you try to keep track and you follow your loved one, going wherever they are taken. Often nobody's got a clue what's going on, only those families who are a few steps ahead of you. They've been where you are.

CARDS, LETTERS, PRESENTS AND RULES

Letter writing can become obsessive because letters are often the only time you'll be able to be true to yourself. I've been known to write up to 20 pages and multiple Valentine cards.

There are strict rules when it comes to the kind of cards you can send through the system, but you'll only know these through other people telling you, or your cards being rejected. Letters and cards can be sprayed with spice liquid so in some jails every letter prisoners receive is a photocopy unless sent via card companies with names so crap I'm embarrassed to say them out loud. There's a company called Jailmate Cards – I appreciate that they exist, but it's not really my bag – they are either 'Naughty girls love naughty shoes and naughty boys' and sad-faced mugshots of teddy bears. These cards really take away the magic of it all – the smell, the touch ... Even if you send a baby scan the original won't be let through in a lot of prisons these days: he will be given a scan of a scan of your womb that's been approved by censors.

If you send a painting by a child, most of the time it won't get through. Some letters and drawings using felt tips won't be accepted either. Raised images with sticky tabs, things stuck onto the card, glitter, ribbons, badges, padded, none of this will get through.

PHONES

Most people don't know the most basic fact: you can never call your partner, they can only call you. With all the bad stories about prisons in the news, when he doesn't ring the worrying will make you physically sick. Often the phone credit runs out for days because it's hard when you want to forget time and really connect. How do you know if they're OK? You simply don't. One way round this is a mobile phone and through emotional desperation, a lot of Prison Wives smuggle them in. If you get caught, it can add time to their sentence and even get you a sentence of your own so don't get pushed into it question if it's worth it.

Most mornings, Elliot calls to tell me he's safe and well, to talk about plans for the day and arrange when we will speak next. If I'm expecting to hear from him but I don't then all kinds of things will go through my head. It's worse still when my phone battery dies. I've bought several new battery packs to prevent this happening – another boring tool in my prison survival kit.

Some prisons have phones built into the cells and this is a good thing for privacy. Phone sex can be a bit awkward if the phones are on the landings. Sorry to be straight up, but the intensity and frustration comes in waves. You desire everything from their aroma to their ... I'll cut myself off, like the prison phone cuts you off.

The most memorable cut-off was when we were cut off when my mum died. I was in a complete mess, desperately needed to talk for ten times longer than we could, but in full flow of tears – BEEP – 'You have 30 seconds remaining' – and he was gone. Prisoners can go to the chaplaincy and they might be able to help with a call, but it's never the hug you so badly need in these types of circumstances.

SUPPORT IN THE OUTSIDE WORLD

Well, first of all I should say there's very little from the system. If you need to know anything, the prison won't be there to help you.

A very good resource can be social media groups. Often the biggest questions you have are age-old and you'll meet people who know exactly the right answer, and who are unafraid and unembarrassed to discuss the issue. This is the obvious benefit of the internet, when it goes well – you can get the things you need (support, advice, love) without the trappings of the real world (judgements, classism, nastiness, rumours).

Before being accepted into a group, there are set rules and set questions. Most groups are private due to paranoia and press. And as soon as your request is accepted, you'll encounter the rules set by the admins.

You'll have to answer some basic questions to show you're authentic, then the Admins or Moderators will approve or decline your request to join their group. The best admins and moderators are people who have had at least a year's experience in the system. They will have experienced many prisons, many different sets of rules. Some groups have a high turnover of members due to the instability of relationships, mental health, or because people have come to the end of their journey. And yet often people return to the group if their loved one has reoffended.

I should also warn you that sometimes it doesn't go well – Prison Wives can have a mob mentality, you put a step wrong and you'll be kicked out without warning – the way some women intimidate, patronise and assert authority is like the prison system has rubbed off on them. I've often seen admins' state: 'This is MY group, and you will obey MY rules'. There are some incredibly supportive groups; they'll be there for you all hours, they get you and you become an online family. These groups are made up of people who are hurting. All Prison Wives are welcome unless you're supporting a sex offender, animal cruelty offender and most of all, anything to do with crimes against children. Anyone supporting drug dealers, addicts, murderers, armed robbers and fraudsters is welcome. You won't be judged.

Then there are the groups that are known as 'Prison Wives After Dark'. For these women, sex is all they can think about. For the sake of those who don't want the constant obsessive sex memes in their face, the after-dark groups are kept separate from the main support groups.

These groups are full-on, way above top-shelf. Let's start with the photos. After a while in a system that totally lacks privacy, most partners just stop caring who sees their nude photos or hears their phone sex. Unless you're talking about 'I'm gonna dress you as Pikachu then walk you round Lidl on a lead' then I'm sure officers get bored of seeing and hearing the same old smut.

You could send images of yourself in an explicit pornographic pose to one prison wife I knew and she would superimpose you into a starry sky, with your legs spread wide across the night sky. You'd only see the image if you were to squint. It was one way to bypass the security checks in the post room. Prison Wives become well acquainted with photo censoring and editing techniques. As I said before – heart-shaped peg, cell-shaped hole lined with barbed wire.

MOVING TOWARDS RELEASE

In Cat-D prisons the security is lessened and so are the stresses. My partner Elliot described standing there and looking through the metal fence at the countryside beyond as one of the happiest moments of his life. I remember him excitedly telling me, 'You can have as much toilet roll as you want, and that it's there free on the landing!'

Then next step is day release. For those with partners and the financial capability, you'll probably end up going straight to a budget hotel. I've tried making those rooms romantic by temporarily sticking cheap wallpaper (with roses on it) to the door, buying fairy lights, fruit and a plant. You learn to be resourceful at Poundland.

Then prisoners get home leave: it starts as two nights, then three, then four. They receive a travel warrant, which takes the financial pressure off you. For home leave they are allowed to bring some clothes and they are trusted to carry a small amount of belongings. It's going to be hard for them returning after two, three or four nights together, but it'll be worth it. You'll get to hold each other through the night, wake up together and do it all again, three times! Some days, you'll stay in bed having sex and looking at each other. You're not actually meant to admit this; you'll have to say on the day release forms that you're using this time wisely, for finding work and 'strengthening family ties'. Well, sex is a part of bonding, so why should we hide it?

COSTS

You are going to have to adapt to this new life, because having a loved one in prison can be expensive and there won't be much of a warning or time to save up for it. You may have lots of new responsibilities and you could end up looking after the family without your loved one. They may have left debts left behind, a mortgage, car insurance and their side of the bills to cover. You may have to change jobs or sell your car. Belongings may be taken from you on a confiscation order. Finances and childcare can cause trouble on the outside. Add a prison sentence with a sprinkle of bitterness and a splash of resentment into the mix and you've got more than a huge concrete wall to get over. But you can do it if you work at it together. Here's an example of one Prison Wife's monthly costs: I spend £100 on fuel, £45 on accommodation, as he is very far away, £40 on food and expenses, £9 on stamps, £25 for his canteen shopping and £15 on topping up his Prison Voicemail app. Supporting a prisoner can be extremely expensive.

Seeing happy couples connecting by holding hands or even arguing in the town centre makes me so resentful, reminding me of the massive wall between me and Elliot. For sure, he committed a crime – but many crimes shouldn't be punished by imprisonment. People can be helped in far better ways that actually address the core underlying issues, which so often involve psychological illnesses or addictions. Prison tears apart communities and families, whether you're a prison wife, a prison husband, a prison daughter, a prison neighbour or even a prison officer.

HAVING A PARENT IN PRISON

DARCEY HARTLEY ON HAVING A PARENT IN PRISON

It is estimated that 200,000 children are affected by parents being imprisoned across England and Wales. In Scotland alone 30,000 children face parental imprisonment every year. Although the figures are very high, this is never spoken about. My name is Darcey Hartley and I am 16 years old. For 14 years now my dad has been in prison on an IPP sentence.

WHAT IS AN IPP SENTENCE?

IPP (Imprisonment for Public Protection) and DPP (the same but for young offenders) was a sentence established in 2005. They were introduced for those who were a danger to the community (at the time estimated to be approximately 900 prisoners) but instead they were handed out to a shocking 9,000 people.

You are given your 'tariff' and then you are eligible for release if the parole board considers you safe to be in the community. They judge you on your behaviour in prison, which is so far from the real world because it's so packed with drugs and violence. To get released, people were required to complete courses that were not even provided in their particular prison – in other words, the government is locking people up (often for minor crimes) but then not proving a way for them to get out of prison.

IPP was abolished in 2012 but some people are still serving past their tariff. One of these people is my dad. He robbed someone to fund his drug habit. He was given two years 11 months. We thought he would be home in 2007, but that wasn't the case: he's been in for 14 years at this point.

My dad committed the robbery that put him in prison as part of his drug problem – he has addiction issues but he is not a bad person. I've never met anyone as kind and caring, and he would do anything to help anybody. He's so loving, warm-hearted and affectionate. He's my idol; he made mistakes like we all do, but he has changed. Dad has taught me so much and for that, I'm so grateful. Right now, in 2019, he should be at home with us.

Growing up with a dad in prison has been one of the hardest things you could ever imagine. Although we children go through so much every day, the struggles we face are never spoken about. We are never noticed. Through the 13 years Dad has been away it hasn't been easy, and every day we face the same struggles, never even knowing when they are going to end. We would not be able to cope with this journey if it wasn't for strength and determination.

From waking up in the morning until falling asleep at night, it is a constant wait for the phone calls that are the only form of communication we have on a daily basis. Phone calls are so expensive therefore Dad can't always call home, and this would probably be the same for your dad too. On days we don't receive calls we automatically worry, because anything can happen in an environment like prison. It's scary. Phone calls only last 10 minutes and then they cut off, and with five of us to get through on the call, ten minutes is nothing at all. We all have so much to say. Luckily, at the prison Dad is at now they have the 'email a prisoner' reply service.

Even though Dad has been in prison the majority of my life he has always done everything in his power to remain an amazing parent but I just wish he could be sat at home on the sofa with me, helping me with my homework in person rather than over the phone. But I can't sit and think about it too much, or it will do my head in. Because his being here isn't an option for us for us at the moment but I'm grateful for what I do have, even though my heart is broken. I miss growing up without him here as a role model. In my whole 16 years of being alive, my dad's taken me to school twice, to the doctor's once and he's never been to a parents' evening. He has only been to one of my hospital appointments and, if it wasn't for the messed-up system, he would have been there to support me.

Inside the prison Dad has applied for a couple of different courses (such as Victim Awareness and Thinking Skills), yet he hasn't been put on any of them, and he has also been writing to outside agencies to get in-cell courses. He has also been trying to get work in the prison kitchens, because he loves cooking, but so far he has only been able to work in a brew bag workshop (Dad puts sugar, tea and coffee into bags). How is that going to help him prepare for the outside world?

In prison people take advantage of IPPs, asking them to hold things in their cell for them because getting a nicking for drugs or a phone is much better than possibly getting a nicking for fighting if they refuse to do it – any violence makes it very difficult to get release, even if the IPP prisoner didn't start the fight. IPPs are treated differently in prison as they have so much to lose, they just get brushed to one side by officers. I have been on visits before and the way officers have spoken to my dad has really upset me. They speak to him like he is nothing. He is a husband, a son, a brother, an uncle and most importantly, he is my dad.

His current prison is exactly 121.8 miles from home and it's a four-hour round trip for us.

Visiting is scary at first but all you have to remember is you are there to see the person you love and miss more than anything, and nothing else matters. We sit and wait, belly full of butterflies. Once your number is shouted, you go over and an officer pats you down, and sometimes there are sniffer dogs too. It's over and done with very quickly and it's nothing to be nervous about. Then there are the big doors to the visit room and you can see all of the prisoners sat there waiting. I try and spot Dad through the door every time. As soon as they open, I go over to give him the biggest hug. We're finally together – for two hours, that is. Any nerves have disappeared.

There are some nice prison officers who make you feel calm but there's some who make you feel really anxious. On some prison visits, the way officers have made me feel has made me not want to go back. Officers can make you feel intimidated by always staring and there have been a couple who have made comments about my junior arthritis. They have a stair lift, which I need to use because of my condition and for the past couple of visits it hasn't been working so walking up the stairs has caused me bad pain. Mum phoned up about the stair lift and they've said to ring three days prior to my next visit and, if it's still broken, then it's down to my mum whether she decides to bring me or not. That is not fair: why should I have to miss out on seeing my dad because of my disability and because of something that is the prison's fault? On some visits I've sat and cried because I've been in pain and sitting on the floor is better than on the hard chairs in the visit room. I get upset to leave too. I hate leaving Dad behind and, even after 14 years, as soon as the doors close behind me, my heart breaks and I want to cry.

Some days at school I feel like I'm in jail. Does your mind ever run away with itself no matter where you are because you're thinking of the prison life? Teachers tell you what you can and can't do; they are in control, just like the officers. But there's an end to the school day and prison is 24 hours a day, every day, and Dad doesn't know when it will end.

Dad has a lot of good times, times when he is clean. I couldn't be more proud of him for always trying his best. The time leading up to parole is always really stressful, but having a parole date makes us happy and we have hope. Two paroles ago, Dad was doing well and he was clean, so we were expecting him to be released to rehab. Parole day came but the hearing was adjourned out of the blue. Dad felt the rug had been pulled from under his feet and he relapsed on spice. He was then put onto Basic for being under the influence. It is so cruel, how can being locked up 23 hours a day be humane? How can Dad be strong if they're taking phone credit and visits away? They don't only punish Dad, they punish us.

When Dad's parole hearing finally came around, it all went well and we found out he was going to rehab. Words cannot even describe how happy we were. Finally, we saw the light at the end of this dark tunnel. When Dad was released to rehab he progressed so much – he was doing amazingly and every Saturday, we could spend five hours with him, 1pm to 6pm. We would laugh, take photos, go on walks and Dad even cooked for us – he made chicken kebabs. I remember we sat outside the rehab altogether, we were so happy. On those Saturdays we made so many memories. We went into the supermarket to do some shopping once and Dad was buying a new frying pan, he cooked a lot at the rehab, and on the counters they have the Age 25 signs for buying alcohol. Dad thought that meant because his pan was under £25 he couldn't pay there, it was really funny. He hadn't been out for a while so we had to help him with little things like that. But after rehab, he was recalled to prison, even though he had been doing so well. They took him away again.

IN THE OUTSIDE WORLD

All of my friends have always been very supportive so I wouldn't say there's any stigma against me being a child of a prisoner. Friends ring me to see how things are going and how Dad is doing and continue to tell me he will be home soon. We campaign against IPP sentences and some of my friends have even been on a couple of protests with us and they've shared Dad's petition multiple times. It's really good to have supportive friends, people you can talk to.

I've known Dad's prison number off by heart for years. To his friends he is Ian, to the prison he is A9567AF; to me he is Dad, the best dad. I can't explain the pain you feel in your heart when you know someone you love more than anything is in a place like prison – some of you will be able to relate to me. Dad going back to prison has affected me massively. I suffer with panic attacks and the majority of the time I feel down. Even if Mum is calling the probation officer I struggle to stay in the car without panicking and getting myself upset. I just want them to say my dad can come home now, but I know they won't. I have everything crossed for the next parole and being positive is key throughout these journeys – always remember that.

Prison TV shows affect me really differently – other people can watch them without worries but if I see a fight going on in prison on TV, it sticks in my head and I get scared, thinking the same things happen where Dad is. I can't explain the pain you feel in your heart when you know someone you love more than anything is in a place like that – some of you will be able to relate to me.

The way the news talks about prisoners is disgusting. Not all prisoners are the same and people need to understand that. Some people are in for mistakes they've made and while some are there because they should be, some are there when they shouldn't be! The whole system is a mess.

EMOTIONAL IMPACT AND THE FUTURE

Mum has a Dad smile, that's what I call it – a smile that only Dad can put on her face. She missed him like crazy. We have photos of him up all over the house and when Mum comes in my room. I always catch her staring at the photos of Dad and smiling. I've never seen a love stronger than theirs and they deserve to be together. I wish I could heal the pain she feels on a daily basis, but it's too severe.

No support is offered from the prison or the government – I think they forget how much it really affects the children. I set up a Facebook page not long ago offering support to HMP children. I also sent packs to them so they could write to their dads inside as I know it can be hard for some families, because of how expensive it can be.

Despite everything, I never envy people with both a mum and dad living at home because just because he's in prison it doesn't mean he isn't amazing. But sometimes when I'm out and I see dads and daughters together it does upset me because I wish that was me and mine, being able to be outside together even for the simplest thing, like going for a walk.

All I can say to you is take a day at a time and to let all of your emotions you if you can. You're strong enough to get through this and your parents will be so proud of you.

And I'm only one of the 200,000 children this is currently happening to.

BEING A CHILD IN PRISON

The Truth, from a Confused Young Man by Jon Gulliver

So I first came to prison when I was 14. I was given a DPP sentence (an indeterminate sentence for under-18s). I was sent to a Secure Training Centre, which in my opinion is like a children's home, though you can't come and go as you please. There are a fewer fences and fewer people on your wing than a normal prison. When

I was 16 I got moved to a YOI (Young Offender Institution) – see, when you come to prison, you are always called 'youths' or 'young offenders', but never 'children'. Young Offender Institutions should really be called Kids' Jails (KJs) 'cause as far as age or personality you are still a kid, no matter what crime has been committed.

I feel that it is important to give you a little understanding about the difference in children's jails and adult jails. If you know about teenagers and you know about prison and you combine the two, then you should know what's going to happen – kids often don't give a fuck, so it is a lot rougher in children's jails. Whereas in adult jail it is more of you have a fight and then it's done and that is almost never the case in children's jails – people hold major grudges. There are also a lot more gangs, which in turn leads to more trouble and things becoming even more dangerous and violent.

One place I spent time was Feltham. All the wings are named after birds (albatross, heron, curlew and all the rest) and if you look from a bird's-eye view, the prison is in the shape of an eagle. It is right next to Heathrow airport, so you can hear planes, but you are locked up 23 hours a day. You feel so far yet so close to freedom – it can be a head-fuck.

Criminal responsibility in England starts at age ten, but to be put in a YOI, you have to be at least 15, and you can stay there until you are 21. But

if you are a dickhead and kicking off all the time and causing nuff problems, they can 'star you up' (this is when you are put into a jail for people older than you).

When you first go into YOI you have a lot of people who think they are the man, Jack-the-lad, think they know everything. But you are in for a quick culture shock as when you go onto the wing, there are a whole lot of other people who have the same mindset. You will see so many different types of people – some look like they are too young to be in prison – some of those kids look about 40 'cos they've been smoking crack and heroin for years. You think to yourself, 'Wow, my man must've had a hard life!' What it also showed me is that there is always someone who is worse off than you.

When you go to prison, they will tell you 'We are here to help you, we are here to help rehabilitate you, we are here to show you how responsible adults should act' – but that isn't the case. So I feel that it is important to explain a bit about what it is like to essentially grow up in prison – if you ever do fully 'grow up'. There are so many things that you go through. Like, what do you want to do when you are older? How do you want your life to be? What will your role be in society? But for me, as I was on an indeterminate sentence, the fact that I may not ever get out of prison made it hard for me to even think about those things. Whenever I did, it would just make me think about what I was missing. And how can you even think about what you want to do and who you want to be when you do not even know when you are getting out? And to be brutally honest, the longer I spent in jail, the more painful it felt to think about those things. Not only that, but it was scary to think about what life would be like when I got out as I had become so used to being in prison.

When you are growing up, you want a sense of independence. And you want to be able to rebel, just like any normal person who is growing up. But in prison, you are not able to do that: you are in an environment that by definition restricts you. That is a hard thing to come to terms with. And while normal kids are out with their friends or playing football or riding their bike, and are able to release all that testosterone, you have no outlet. All you have is sitting in your cell 23 hours a day. You can feel like a lion banged up in a cage all day.

Yo G, listen, you are going to have a lot of time on your hands. And there is a lot of boredom. And at times there will be a lot of tension on the wing as, like anywhere, if you put a load of people together who have all got their own problems and nowhere to go, then what do you expect? That is why it is important to find other things to do (i.e. like, paint-by-numbers, listening to music, exercising, making phone calls, matchstick modelling). If you don't, then all you are going to do is sit there and think and think – and all that is going to lead to is you getting yourself in trouble. Yeah, there are things like pool and table tennis, but those things will only occupy you for so long. And when you are on your own with just your thoughts, you can do a lot of overthinking. And often that doesn't lead you to a good place.

When you are young, one of the big challenges you face is body image. So, you go to the gym to look good. 'Cause if you look good, then you feel good. But in prison, you also go to the gym to get big as a way to show that you are not a victim and that you can look after yourself. You have that added pressure of always having to look macho.

Listen, bro, let me tell you what it is when it comes to women. Now you will see a lot of female members of staff. You will get some who will have a little flirt with you. And don't get me wrong, as a young man, when you've got a woman showing you some attention, it is nice. The bottom line is yes, you are a man, and yes, you have needs, but just be careful what you do and how you act around women in prison.

Remember, the only thing in that department that you can one hundred per cent rely on while you are in prison is your right hand.

In prison, there is no talk about how you should treat women. It is just about objectifying them. Good-looking body, big tits, big bum, whatever it is. You are not taught manners. You are not taught how you should look after a woman. So for me, because I came to jail young, I had never been on a date with a woman. I'd never asked a woman out and now, as a 27-year-old man, I'm sitting there sometimes and thinking to myself, 'How the hell am I going to ask someone on a date? What do you do, what don't you do?' And there's another big issue in prison: you are told to see people in a certain way in jail. You are not allowed to care for people, and people are not allowed to care for you – it is seen as 'inappropriate'. But when you get out, you need to interact with people differently. For anyone just leaving the prison system, that is hard. So how do you think it is for someone who has *grown up* in the prison system? It's worth thinking about. You are expected to know what's right and wrong. But how on earth can you know right from wrong if you've never been taught? Because what is deemed 'appropriate' or 'inappropriate' in prison is not necessarily the same on road.

So I came into prison a confused young child, and I've come out of prison a confused young man. I've left knowing what is right from wrong in terms of committing crime, but not really having a clue of how to socialise with society in a respectable manner.

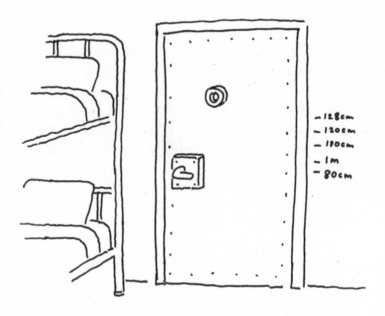

Being in prison at a young age can give you a complete mistrust of people. You have no understanding of how to talk to people 'cause the way you talk to people in prison and the way you would talk to people on road is completely different. And just the way that you see people. If all you see is people telling you what to do and what not to do, and not to even have a normal conversation with you, then what hope do you have when you get out into the big wide world?

It is important to talk about loneliness as it is something that you will definitely experience in prison. People may say that you are on a wing with a load of other people, and there are staff there all the time, so you're never 'alone'. But there have been times when I have been around my mates and we are having a laugh, but there is just this emptiness inside. It is not a nice feeling and it can lead to some dark thoughts.

And that leads me on to self-harm in prison. Now I have done this myself and it is a big issue. I remember once, before I was due to go on my visit, the alarm went and loads of staff were running around. And my visit was late because of it. So when I came back, I asked the member of staff what had happened. It turned out that one of my friends had tried to self-harm. 'Will he be coming back later?' I asked, as I thought he had gone to hospital. And I still remember to this day, the officer turned around and said to me, 'He will not be coming back. He has killed himself.' This fucked with my head as a family member of mine had killed themselves as well, so it brought all that back up for me. And you don't get any mental health support from the prison.

In my opinion, growing up in prison is like planting a seed in concrete. You never have the opportunity to grow. Now don't get me wrong, you will have changed in terms of how you look. But the things that matter, emotionally and mentally ... I am just the same as that 14-year-old boy that walked through those gates over 12 years ago.

CARING FOR A CHILD IN PRISON

JULIA'S STORY

Having children when you are in prison is by far the hardest and most soul-destroying part of the whole experience. I was whisked away from my children suddenly and had not prepared for it well at all.

I was very fortunate that I had a support network at home, who could take care of my two daughters in my absence – the reality is that many women do not have this and their children are taken into care.

When you are faced with the fact that you may be going to jail, or you land there suddenly, you need to quickly make the decision of what you are going to tell your children. My biggest fear was that they would feel abandoned, confused and unloved. Did they think I had just run off by choice? I made the decision with my family and friends to tell them the truth, without going into all the gory details: 'Mummy has made a mistake and will be away for a little while, but she loves you and misses you more than the world.' Tears came to my eyes as I'm writing these words then, even though time has passed. Other women told their children they were working away and even stuck to this during visits, or some chose not to see their children at all while they were in prison. I suppose you need to do the right thing for you, your children and your situation.

If you are only away for a few weeks and your children are young, maybe saying nothing will work for you. I was inside too long to lie and my children were too old to be deceived. Being as honest as I could worked for me. I had already destroyed their trust in my eyes, so being honest was the only option. My daughters have learnt from the experience too. They could quite easily be deemed as 'damaged', but I see them as well-rounded individuals, who are non-judgemental and can empathise with others. My youngest daughter is an advocate for injustice of any kind and it is heart-warming to see her genuine passion for inequality and discrepancies in so-called justice.

My children's love and respect for me never faltered, and they were still proud of me, even though I deemed myself worthless. I hated myself for what I had done to them, the guilt ripped me apart and still does. Use this guilt to give you strength and to make sure that you never end up in this position again. Your children are often stronger than you are – that is something to remember. It was me that cried endlessly day after day for the first couple of months. My every waking and sleeping thought was of my children, what a bad mum I was, how I wished I could turn back time and undo everything I had ever done.

The first visit I had was the worst. I cried uncontrollably throughout the full two hours, gripping onto my six-year-old little girl, not wanting to ever let her go. When the time came for them to leave, I cried for days on end. I can't explain the pain I felt to you now, although I know it will haunt me forever. I was lucky that, on top of my normal visits, we had family visits. It was completely different to the normal visits – you could play with them normally, walk round the visits hall, read with them and have that one-to-one contact that is so important to you.

Sending your children letters and cards is a great way for you to keep in contact with them. It's a lovely surprise for them, to come home from school and find there is something from Mummy waiting. I spent all my phone credit ringing them, or ringing about them. I loved getting photos from them and plastering them next to my bed. Although looking at photos of them at first is hard, you learn to appreciate every little thing you took for granted before. My cell became a shrine to my children, not only covered in photos, but pictures they had drawn. I managed to collect bits and bobs and decorated the wall with fairy lights, fairy wings and ribbons. The funny thing is your cell or room ends up looking like a child's bedroom. 'Story Book Dads/Mums' is available at most prisons and you get to record a story or a message, which gets edited before being made into a CD and sent to your child. Don't worry if you think you are going to sound rubbish, they cut the bad bits out. With me, it would take ages as I used to sob uncontrollably about anything related to my kids.

Birth Companions is an excellent charity supporting pregnant women and new mothers behind bars. Some female jails have Mother and Baby Units that are accessible for women who

are going to have/already have children under the age of 18 months old. Of course, there are various risk assessments and multi-agencies involved and each case is judged on its merits. Only ladies with what is deemed as 'exceptional behaviour' are allowed on the Mother and Baby unit – no slip-ups allowed, model behaviour only! This excludes a lot of women, which is a frustration for many and there are only a certain amount of spaces available.

In these units mums sleep in the same room as their children – parental responsibility is still held by Mum, not the prison. Each mother is allocated a case worker, whose job it is to help Mum build confidence and develop parenting skills. This support can often feel like surveillance. Grit your teeth – and ride through it. It is temporary and very soon you will be home with your baby.

When babies are old enough – at eight weeks – they attend morning nursery while their mothers work in the prison or are in education. Eight weeks seems very young to leave your baby for the day and can be heartbreaking. In the real world how many mums return to work when their baby is only eight weeks old? We must remember it is jail – not the real world – but we have real-life emotions and natural instincts that are often forgotten or ignored.

Mothers return at lunchtime to feed and change their babies before spending the afternoon in parenting classes, learning a range of skills, from cooking and budgeting to play techniques and baby massage. They can also shop for their babies in the prison's baby shop, using money they've earned from working in the prison. I remember the girls were allowed to order goods from ASDA for the babies, but often got ambiguous items for themselves that they would share with us! I can remember tucking into a Farley's rusk once, thinking it was better than the slop being served up for dinner!

Babies are taken out of the prison two to three times a week. They go on trips, such as to local children's centres, so least baby gets a taste of the real world. Children can also be allowed time on home visits, while Mum stays in the prison. This gives opportunities to form relationships with partners and other family members. If Mum is eligible for home leave, then she and baby can start to resettle back at home before it's time to wave goodbye to the prison for good.

Some officers are really understanding if you have kids – you will know which ones will help you and which ones won't!

L G B T Q +

BY SARAH JANE BAKER AS TOLD TO CARL CATTERMOLE

The anxiety facing someone preparing for prison can be extreme, but when issues of sexuality are added into the mix you might also ask yourself whether you'll be beaten up, raped, murdered or prostituted.

When I first went to prison back in 1985 gay prisoners had their cells burnt out; they were beaten, stabbed, slashed with razor blades, and some of them had boiling water poured over their heads. Other prisoners would applaud the senseless violence and the prison officers would often stand by and let it pass (at that time some prison officers would also wear National Front badges on their uniform).

Fast forward thirty years and things have improved, but it's still a very hostile environment for LGBTQ+ people. If you have 'come out' in the outside world then coming out in prison is like doing it all over again. Staying in a cell and being in the closet can be doubly tough: showing love to someone in the visit room is a no–go, and amorous phone calls and letters are monitored by staff and that information has been known to filter through to people on the wing.

However, many of the estimated 15,000 prisoners identifying as LGBTQ+ find themselves really well-supported and loved. On many wings you will find openly 'out' prisoners – Ronnie Kray is just one famous example. The LGBTQ+ experience is so vast that I can't hope to represent it all here. I can only talk from my own experience, but for many more points of view you can read the Bent Bars newsletter available online.

Many men, though they may be married outside of jail, have made the choice to be gay for the stay, sometimes paying gay or trans–women for sex with drugs money or private cash, and some are even in long–term relationships. In shared cells prison staff are powerless to prevent prisoners from finding comfort in each others' arms – love is more powerful than prison rules and lust is even more powerful than loneliness.

The culture of homophobia mostly comes from petty 'badboys'. The irony is that over the years I've been good friends with some of the big time gang-sters they look up to – and those people have much bigger things to think about than how another per-son expresses their love. Meanwhile, the petty talk endlessly about phones and drugs in your arse – batty boy this, faggot that – I've heard more about arse in here than I have in a gay nightclub.

In this climate, you often have to fight tooth and nail even though you really don't want to, just to protect yourself. This leads to nickings, which can have obvious knock–on effects for your sentence and parole.

TRANSGENDER

Upon entry to prison, unless you provide a Gender Recognition Certificate showing you are already being treated for gender dysphoria, the prison can say that you're making a 'lifestyle choice'. The press officer for the Prison Officers Association's view is that 'some trans prisoners are genuinely gender dysphoric, others are looking at it as a soft option for prison life' and in some senses I wouldn't disagree – but if constant bullying, comments, sexual harassment and isolation are your idea of a 'soft option' then I'd suggest you haven't really thought things through.

It's true that, according to the rules, trans prisoners should have access to resources like private washing and laundry, but the reality is that prisons are so understaffed you will often have to wash your clothes in your cell's sink and you will often be unable to shower for days because there's no member of staff available to unlock you. There is another rumour that you're more likely to achieve parole if you are trans, but that is poppycock.

Wanting to transition is something that comes from so deep within but, like anything in prison, it needs to be bureaucratically approved. You'll have to change your name by deed poll then apply to the Governor for name change, make a Change Of Clothing application, inform HMRC, MoJ and the police, and then you sit and wait for your first GIC appointment.

You'll be referred to a Gender Identity Clinic (GIC) by the prison doctor or psychiatrist but you probably won't get given an appointment date immediately, if at all, as the NHS capacity is so small. Often, you'll just hear a knock on your door and have a minute to get dressed up and made up, as a clinician will be waiting and will expect to see you present in your desired gender. You'll have to tell them your life story: from your crimes to your childhood to your historical sexual experiences, all within earshot of a prison officer.

When it comes to hormones, if you start to transition whilst inside you'll likely have to 'live in the role' for over two years before a GIC clinician will prescribe them. The Clinic denied me a diagnosis of gender dysphoria until I took the very extreme step of removing my own testicles with a prison razor blade. I'm not going to go into it all here – if you'd like to know more, you can buy my book.

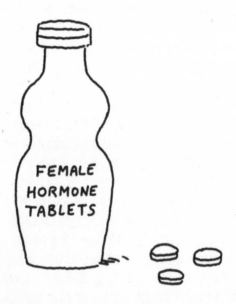

I transitioned genders not because I want an 'easy ride'. I did it because I had to. The issue dominates my life, sometimes because of my own self–understanding, but more often because straight, cis-gendered people preach at me before they know the first facts about my life or the scenario within which I live. Anyway, I'm not here to give my tranifesto, I'm here to talk about prison issues.

In this place, it seems half the men want to ignore me, half want to fight me, half want to fuck me. Do the maths – many men want to do all three, but such is life in the jailhouse. I don't use political correctness as a weapon against prison staff or other prisoners. I tried to retain a sense of humour and have embraced the trans–phobia that I encounter frequently in the spirit of forgiveness or at least understanding. I am aware of how I stand out in a male prison, especially if I am wearing my skirt and Ugg boots. I am often told that is my own fault that I am attacked, as many people that I encounter still believe that being transgender is no more than a lifestyle choice. Of course, these opinions will continue as long as the right–wing press and media continue to promote them. For those journalists and their readers, for whom gender is the least of their worries, it is incredibly cruel to provoke the country to mess with the mental health of those whose gender is such an important and sensitive subject. Transgender mental health is often bad even within the community, but when you're in a hostile environment like prison it's a living hell.

As a prisoner, I have no access to the emotional support that a trans–woman could receive in the wider community. A practical solution is to write as much as possible. If you're short of people to communicate with then Bent Bars run an excellent pen pal partner service geared towards LGBTQ+ prisoners. One of my most important sources of relief has been writing to other serving trans prisoners who really understand what we go through.

Heels over 2.5 inches are generally not allowed behind bars in case they're used as a weapon. And whether or not you're allowed a wig or hairpiece depends on the governor. Legally you haven't got a right to this, but some governors may give you the option. I looked like one of the Two Ronnies in drag when I first started transitioning, but by gleaning advice from various females (visitors, chaplains and screws) and reading make-up books ordered in from the library and practicing my technique, I am now a looker.

A **trans man** is a person who was born female and has transitioned to become male. This often gets less attention than the male–to–female transition. To the best of my knowledge, no past or present discourse on transgender prisoners has considered any of the issues faced by trans men prisoners held in both the male or female estates. They are a significant group of prisoners that seem to be ignored by the Ministry of Justice and the prison system as a whole. The trans-men that I have been in contact with over many years tell me that they feel as if their emotional needs are neglected because without a penis, they are not legally recognised as men until they possess a Gender Recognition Certificate. Most trans men choose the 'safe' option, to be housed in the female estate, for it is believed that female prisons are less hostile to transgender prisoners than male prisons. This generalisation may indeed be true regarding the risk of violent attack, but does not take account of the discrimination that they can face from prisoners who feel that such people are an abomination to God. There are hate-filled prisoners in both male and female estates.

There are currently 42 transgender women in female prisons, but there are rumours of plans to move some of them back because the prison authorities omitted to make the required risk assessment on a male prisoner who claimed to be transgender before being moved to a female prison, where they sexually assaulted a female prisoner. The fallout and consequences of this prisoner's behaviour has been felt throughout the transgender community with all transfers to female prison being stopped.

As uncomfortable as it may make people feel, I cannot avoid mentioning the 80+ prisoners serving sentences for rape against women or children, who identify as trans. I should be careful about applying such a judgement, but there are a small number of manipulative 'trans–fakers'. Neither of these groups should be used to judge or discriminate against other people whose identity overlaps with theirs.

Any prisoner who has had the pleasure of meeting me during the last 30 years will no doubt be surprised that, when it comes to the management of transgender prisoners I have much sympathy for the Ministry of Justice, because it is a total minefield. However there are a number of governors who are strongly opposed to accommodating transgender prisoners in their jails, and they are often supported by right–wing media or religious fundamentalist organisations.

Trans people seem to be on the bottom rung of the social pecking order. Trans–phobic comments and attacks are commonplace and few prisoners are ever held to account for their discrimination as staff, on the whole, seem reluctant to get involved and intercede on our behalf.

Through my eyes and those of many of my trans–sisters, most prison officers do not appear to have any malicious intent towards us but I would suggest that they lack both the training and confidence needed to deal with transphobia in prisons. Coming from a childhood full of abuse both physical and sexual, and raised on the mean streets of south London and three children's homes, even I am taken aback by the increasing level of extreme violence that is becoming the norm on our prison landings.

Since the Brexit vote there has been a noticeable increase in the number of negative comments I have heard from prisoners in this jail – when people voted to 'take their country back', they believe they are no longer need to hide their views on anything. They're selectively reclaiming Britishness – flying the Union Jack but leaving behind values of tolerance and politeness.

Genuine allies are often scared to be seen talking to you in case they are labelled gay by association, so you have even less community protection and become yet more vulnerable. LGBTQ+ prisoners should be careful: they shouldn't leave their door on latch, and should make sure it's locked before going to work, visits or education to prevent prisoners stealing (or transphobes destroying) our few gender–related items and other possessions.

I am luckier than most prisoners in that I have a great support network (Pam, Kelly, Carl and several others), and many family members have embraced my transition after the initial shock, especially when the media covered my story for the first time. I am waiting desperately for parole, which has entered another phase of delays. I try to remain patient although like a graceful swan on the lake, I'm often paddling hard just to stay afloat. To all the prison staff and the kind people who have supported me – I love you and thank you all.

FOREIGN NATIONAL PRISONERS

The question of foreign national prisoners is a complex issue that reaches to the heart of the justice system. Barely any courses are provided in foreign languages and people serving indeterminate sentences for more serious crimes are just deported back to their country as soon as possible – essentially the government doesn't want to help improve these people, it just wants them out. Very few kindnesses are afforded – if you get no visits at all as a foreign national you are given a free call home that lasts a measly five minutes per month.

If you came to England as a refugee then you can be deported if you're given a sentence of over two years. If you are a non-EEA (European Economic Area) citizen then you can be deported if you are given a sentence of 12 months or more. If you are an EEA citizen, you can be deported too but the sentence needs to be slightly longer. And if you're Irish, you can end up in that boat too. If you are a foreign prisoner, you are unlikely to gain D-Cat (an open prison) either.

You can serve part of your sentence in your country of citizenship. There's a thing called the ERS (Early Removal Scheme), where foreign national prisoners can leave the country before their sentence is totally served, or, if you're on an indeterminate sentence, you can leave the UK any time after your 'tariff' is finished. Darcey already mentioned that the government holds people way past tariff because they are considered a risk to the public but it seems none of this applies when it comes to releasing them into other countries.

If any of this applies to you then get proper advice from a lawyer (if legal aid is available) and check the relevant Prisoners' Advice Service information sheets and contact Bail For Immigration Detainees.

In 2008 the Prison Reform Trust and Ministry of Justice made a booklet called *The Prisoners' Information Book*. It's now outdated, however for what it lacks, it's been translated into 27 different languages so may be of great help to foreign nationals looking for basic information.

EDUCATION

Incarceration an is edgy word but the reality is that it makes your mind feel like mush – the education department can be the true antidote to this. Education is often one part self-improvement, one part survival strategy. Get involved as soon as you hit the wing. You can even get paid a tiny amount to attend classes.

It's like a school reunion for the kids who got expelled (1 per cent of the general population get permanently expelled but over 40 per cent of prisoners were). Sitting in a row of rickety seats transports you straight back to school and inevitably some people do still act like kids, totally allergic to the classroom environment, sprawled out and taking the piss (sometimes this is their fault, sometimes the teaching is unengaging and is not dynamic – just like school). Other prisoners look like they're in deep mental revolution – learning maths, learning literature, learning to *learn* when they doubted they ever could. I've personally come across some of the best teachers in my life through prison – educators like Alistair Fruish are prime examples.

After you've taken the basic tests, you'll be able to look at further courses. For a complete list of courses available, your prison should have a 'Directory of Education and Training' available for you to have a look at and *Inside Prison* has a directory that lists all available grants. The most recent edition was published in 2015, but it should still be useful.

Level 1 courses will be mandatory – if you refuse to attend you'll get a nicking. After this comes Level 2 courses, which are equivalent to GCSEs. Once you've got these badges on your towel you'll be allowed into the big pool and will be offered a wider range of courses. Level 3 courses are equivalent to A-levels.

Additionally, there are courses on PowerPoint and courses on business (I used to laugh watching course tutors patronise multi-million pound drug dealers about supply and demand) and citizenship courses where foreign people learn stuff about Britain that no Brit has ever needed to know – 250 obscure historical dates, the height of the London Eye, the approximate square mileage of the Lake District, etc.

Also available may be some vocational courses. However, don't expect them to allow you access to a screwdriver or Stanley knife. These kinds of courses include decorating, bricklaying, food hygiene certificates for kitchen workers and industrial cleaning courses for 'biohazards'.

Some prisons still have an arts education department but so many have been closed that it's become more of a DIY in-cell hobby, so I've given it its own section rather than including it here as part of formalised education.

Apart from the most basic education courses you'll need to pay out your own pocket, apply for funding or get a student loan. Due to various funding cutbacks the amount of people who achieved A-level grade qualifications in prison is 10 per cent of what it was a decade ago. Up until 2012, you could do a degree without fees but now it costs around £15,000: unsurprisingly, uptake has dropped considerably. Funding is also much harder to secure for foreign nationals. For more about student loans for prisoners, see the Prisons Education Trust article on the subject.

People are often moved from jail to jail and courses are not offered in all the prisons, plus providers change from place to place so people are often unable to graduate. For example, Elliot was doing OU psychology but was moved before a crucial test, then he wanted to do addiction therapy, but it wasn't offered in the next jail. Now he's doing plastering and he's not sure if he'll get it completed before he gets moved again.

Prisoners' Education Trust is a charitable body that has been around for years. They operate in every single UK prison and provide distance learning to something like 3,000 individuals every year in subjects both academic and artsy. If you write to them, they'll send you a copy of their Access to Learning programme. Find the address at the back of the book.

Open University is the UK's specialist distance learning provider and it has been educating prisoners for over 40 years. In short, I highly rate them. If you're preparing for a sentence you should get the ball rolling before you go in – it's much easier to get involved without the big prison bureaucracy having to approve every step. Their criminology professor, Dr David Scott, is an end-of-level boss when it comes to UK prison issues. The added bonus of OU courses is that you can study after you've been banged up for the evening, which means people can use this potential dead-time constructively, a total godsend.

Institute of Prison Law operates a course that improves people's knowledge of prison legal affairs. According to their website they have trained hundreds of solicitors, governors and prisoners. It's a distance learning course that you do via the internet if you're on the out, via DVD if you're behind bars. Worth a punt if you've got the cash (it's priced way beyond most people's means; I'd love to see someone offer this stuff to prisoners at an affordable rate).

Learning another language behind bars informally is an amazing way to meet foreign nationals and hear interesting stories about their lives back home and how they ended up doing porridge. I speak OK Spanish, thanks to Arturo, a Columbian grandad *campesino* (bumpkin) who'd hit hard times and tried to bring a suitcase full of cocaine through Heathrow. He didn't speak a word of English before jail and as a result, he didn't understand basic outside-world vocabulary such as 'traffic cone' or 'coat hanger', but he did know about 'avin a bubble' and 'swervin the scoobies'.

Oh, and, how can I forget **the library**? You should be allowed to go once a week. Libraries are run by local authorities: some are extensive and excellent, others have a bookshelf of celeb autobiographies from 2004. You'll find a big waiting list for books by David Icke, Andy McNab and 50 Cent. I saw his autobiography in one prison library and it was so well-read, it looked like a sixteenth-century edition of the Bible.

And one last thing ... the behavioural courses offered in prison. I never had to sit any so I can't give you a review, but on offer you'll find a lot of courses with cranky acronyms – C.A.R.E., D.I.D., R.E.S.O.L.V.E., C.A.L.M., F.O.C.U.S. and (the slightly less catchy) T.V.S.O.G.P. There are too many to start explaining what they all are – see *Inside Time* or ask on the wing.

ART

Prison turns you greyscale: grey tracksuit, scaly grey skin from the crap food and lack of sun, thin grey hair from the stress – you need to find ways to colour yourself back in.

It doesn't matter how much supposed 'talent' or experience you have, a tube of oil paint is one of the cheapest therapies available. I saw with my own eyes sexagenarian (that word means someone in their sixties, not a sex offender) bank robbers on their fifteenth sentence saying they'd found life's true meaning while they painted wonky landscapes. It's primal and pure, so far away from the clattering headache you're surrounded with in that shithole.

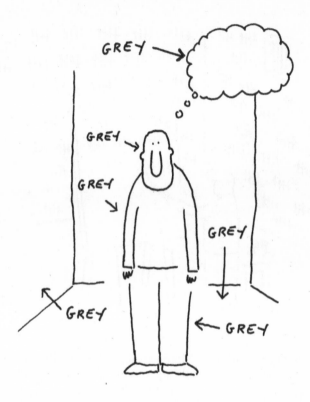

You can buy some basic art materials off the canteen, you can make papier mâché in your cell, and obviously, you can write down your thoughts with a pencil. Since most of the actual arts education in prisons has been defunded, you should be confident to do it on your own steam.

There's an art market of types behind bars – if you're good, you could make enough to live on. Some prisoners do photorealistic portraits, others do these mangled Manga-style drawings of girls, where the body parts connecting the lips, tits and hips are an afterthought, others spend absolutely months making sculptures from

matchsticks and glue. These matchstick creations range from sets of drawers all the way to a full-scale Big Ben (I'm just testing to see if you're still awake).

Sometimes (too rarely!) there are arts events in prison and with ex-prisoners in the community. Organisations like Synergy, Clean Break, Safe Ground, Catch22, Geese Theatre, Odd Arts, Ride Out and Unlock drama do good theatre work. As far as music projects go, there are: Music in Prisons (by the highly recommended Irene Taylor Music Trust), Good Vibrations, Finding Rhythms, Vox Liminis (check out their podcasts too), The Prison Choir Project and Jail Guitar Doors (founded by Billy Bragg) who provide guitars for prisoners. If you'd like to get involved then check what's happening and who works in your local area and if you're inside then ask if anything is operating in your jail. These small organisations often only have the capacity to work in a few jails – they should be properly funded and nationwide.

If you've made a piece of work you're proud of then you should submit it to the Koestler Trust. Every year they give out hundreds of awards and certificates for painting, sculpture, writing, music and performance. You'll get feedback from experts in the field and you can even win money. Go check out their yearly exhibitions and their regular events and give them money, volunteer for them, buy work from them. The *Prison Service Journal* did a complete issue on prison arts in 2018 if you want the long read.

DRUGS

ELLIOT ON DRUGS
(AND GETTING OFF DRUGS)

My name's Elliot and, by the age of 26, I was ten years into a massive addiction to heroin. One thing had led to another and I became a drugs courier to feed my habit, leading me inevitably to getting nicked. The judge took one look at my skinny, ill figure (less heroin chic, more Catweazle with track marks) and remanded me straight to jail.

Arrival

As an addict arriving in prison you can expect to be offered a pharmaceutical substitute to stabilise your physical dependence – something to stop you clucking, basically. You'll be seen by a doctor at reception after a nurse's initial assessment and he or she will prescribe you methadone or Subutex for heroin addiction, or Librium for alcoholism. The amount of methadone they gave me was so small, it just about stopped me pooing my pants as I was using a lot of at the time, so don't expect much initially. You can request to go up in dose at a later date.

Detox Wings

If on a script for a substituting drug, you'll be put onto a detox wing, also called substance mis-use units, or 'junkie wings'. The idea is you're on this wing for the first month or so while your withdrawal symptoms calm down and you can get the help you need. My experience as an addict in prison showed me that prison health-care is pretty rubbish, so don't expect too much.

You're going to be surrounded by dozens of other drug addicts on this wing, so remain cautious. If you leave your cell door open, don't be surprised if you get thieved from. The detox wing is the target audience for dealers in prison. Also, expect people to be exchanging their pre-scription meds constantly with each other. On the menu you'll have 'pregabs' (Pregabalin), 'gabbies' (Gabapentin), any opiate-based drug including Tramadol, Subutex (Buprenorphine) – a blocker, but gets you high if you sniff it, anti-psychotics, Benzos (especially Diazepam) and even paracetamol that can be crushed and mixed with other substances.

NPS

NPS stands for 'new psychoactive substances' and refers to the new kids on the block in the drugs world. These are one of the defining issues of the current prison system. The main NPS is spice which until 2016 was sold legally on the high street. It's a synthetic cannabinoid chemical that is often sprayed onto paper, which is then sold and smoked. People think they're smoking weed, but it's a totally different drug; people are 'going over' (overdosing) every day all over the country. I had a go during the first few months and ended up getting twisted-up by officers and placed in segregation because I thought the officers were vampires that had to be slayed. Steer well clear if you can.

Nicotine

If you're on the outside you will probably never understand how much small things like 'burn' (tobacco) mean to prisoners. When cigarettes were banned in 2017, it was never going to be an easy ride. The phoenix has definitely risen from the ashes – these days, prisoners smoke chamomile tea, nicotine patches and even the plastic backings from these patches. They cut it up into little strips, mix it with a teabag, then use a Bible page as a Rizla. People are nearly dying and coughing blood all over the place because addiction is much stronger than common sense. To maintain a cigarette habit, expect to pay a lot: in many jails, a Rizla costs a quid and a roll-up costs a fiver.

Substance Misuse Workers

It's likely you will be approached by, or get the opportunity to talk to, a substance misuse worker working on behalf of a specialist addiction agencies. Some of the agencies I've encountered are Turning Point, Phoenix Futures, CARATs and Forward Trust (previously, RAPt). Generally, they are all good people to be engaged with and they can help assist you with getting and staying clean. They can also assist with Drug Rehabilitation Requirements for court or rehab placements on leaving prison.

I worked as a peer mentor for a couple of these agencies while in prison after getting clean myself and I've known many guys to start out like this and go on to be offered work placements outside after progressing through the system. So even if you're shivering, sweating, nauseous and irritable upon first encounter with these guys and gals, it's worth engaging with them and accessing their services.

'Meds!'

If you remain on methadone or Subutex after moving from a detox wing, you'll collect your meds each morning, awakened by not only your bubbling guts, but also by an officer unlocking your door, shouting, 'Meds!' Get ready for the methadone Olympics. Every other prisoner on meds will be unlocked at the same time and from what I've witnessed, it can get pretty ruthless in the mad rush to feel the sweet relief of what we used to call 'the green handcuffs' (methadone comes as a syrupy green liquid in a little paper cup). I like to tell people the main reason I stopped taking methadone was to get properly clean, but if I'm honest, I got sick and tired of fighting over who was next in the meds queue – it just felt like I was waiting for a dealer in an alleyway.

Stigma

If you're addicted to drugs, no doubt you will have already experienced a bit of negativity from those not involved in the same scene as you. Let's face it, addicts have got a bad reputation and it's no different in prison. Not only may dealers target you as a customer inside, but other prisoners may treat you with suspicion and hostility if they know you are an addict. I managed to avoid any real issues, but I was ready to stop taking drugs after a couple of months – I saw a lot of guys get into debt, stealing from other prisoners, even selling the TVs in their cells to other prisoners on 'basic' regime with no TVs. It's all down to how you carry yourself – if you don't respect your own existence, nobody else will either.

Connections

As with life outside of prison, the company you keep inside will definitely contribute to how easy you find your time. The old saying goes 'Lay down with dogs, pick up fleas', although you might literally pick up fleas if you stay around certain people in prison long enough. Generally though, if you're locked up as a result of your drug use, you might as well take full advantage of the whole experience and seek out people who won't drag you down further. Believe it or not, there are some good people in our prisons with a lot of knowledge about learning from mistakes – you just have to avoid the ones who choose not to learn. I was ready to try something different in my life and get honest enough to say I needed help, and in my experience the people who always do what they've always done, will always get what they've always got.

I still speak to a couple of recovering addicts I met along the way, but only a couple, mind. The sad fact is only a minority get clean and stay clean, but the beautiful thing is that you can form friendships out of the mutual understanding of surviving the horrors of addiction. You could even have meet-ups, like veterans of a traumatic battle, missing body parts and teeth ... back to life, back to reality.

MANDATORY DRUG TESTING

In jail, way before my time, apparently weed was the drug of choice. Thing is, weed stays in your system for 28 days and heroin and crack flush out much, much quicker. So when MDTs were introduced in the early nineties, they stopped people smoking weed and started them on heroin. After their introduction in 1992, heroin use in Britain TRIPLED.

So when the MDT unit appear on your wing you'll see half the wing run back to their cells and fix their piss by downing litres of water mixed with a certain chemical I won't name here. Everyone passes the piss test with flying colours despite the fact you've seen them smoking something the evening before. If you fail a MDT, you'll end up with a nicking.

ALCoHoL

OK, hooch can taste like mouldy orange juice if you make it badly, or like vodka and orange if you do it well. I generally avoided it; being drunk on the wing never really appealed to me plus it has the potential of making you go blind, but if you really want to try, here's how.

You need a couple of large bottles – squash bottles will do. You get the yeast from brown bread, you can crumble it up and just stick it in the bottle, but you'll have soggy bits of bread floating around in your finished product. If you're a pro, you dry the bread out on the pipes, grind it up, stick it in a sock (a clean one) and immerse this in warm water for five minutes before removing it.

So now you take your yeasty water, add a whole load of sugar and top it up with fruit juice. This is pretty much it. Now you just need to leave it to ferment in the warmest part of your cell.

Don't forget to periodically loosen the lid to let the carbon dioxide out. If you don't, it will explode and coat all of your possessions in stinking hooch.

This process takes up to a week, but if you're a real pro, you use a 'kick' (the sludgy sediment from the bottom of a previous batch) and you can do it over a weekend. Not only does this take less time but also the weekends are a 'non patrol state' – i.e. the screws won't raid you out of the blue, as they can do on a normal weekday.

You can go one step better and make vodka: I only saw one guy doing this the whole time I was inside and he sold it on for £20 for half a litre (a lot of money in prison terms). So you take your hooch – a couple litres or so to make it worthwhile – and stick it in a bucket or a cleaned-out bin. Now here's the tricky bit … you need to suspend a smaller bowl in the middle of the bucket – the easiest way to do this is to drill three holes a centimetre beneath the rim, evenly spaced, in your bucket. Do the same to your bowl and tie pieces of rope so your bowl hangs nicely in the middle. Then take a kettle lead, expose the wires at one end and stick this in the mixture. Now you need to attach a sheet of plastic (a section of bin bag will do) over the top of the entire thing but give it a little bit of slack so it sags in the middle. Use elastic bands or rope to seal it so it's airtight.

Now you need to put ice or the coldest thing you can find on the top of this plastic. Stand back and switch on the power. The kettle lead will heat up the hooch in the big bucket, the alcohol will evaporate then condense when it hits the cold plastic and drip into the smaller bowl. After a few hours you will find your bowl is full of distilled home-brew vodka.

MISCELLANEOUS TIPS

Ok, this section is on a bit of a lighter note. A few miscellaneous bits and bobs and how-tos. I could write a whole book about this stuff but I'm going to try and keep it brief. It goes without saying: I DO NOT ADVISE YOU TO DO ANY OF THIS SHIT. In fact, I advise you NOT TO DO IT. But this is what people do:

LIGHTERS
I told you this would be a lighter note (terrible joke). Lighters used to be available on canteen but since the smoking ban you have to go rogue and risk your life to light your fag – risking your life to light a fag is not what I'd call a Life Hack, but here are the potential ways to quench your nicotine thirst:

Technique 1 is to strip back a prison issue vape – inside, there's a filament and if you touch it with bog roll, you'll get a flame. Another is to use the active element of a kettle – you just have to dismantle the base a little bit.

Technique 2 is known as the 'wallbang' – you stick a bit of pencil graphite in the positive and another bit in the negative or get a plug and sheath back the cable (while it's unplugged, obviously) and then plug it in. Next, you brush a separate bit of metal on the positive then use the spark to light a piece of bog roll – bogs your uncle! You can use the power cable to your TV (depends which you want more – a fag or *EastEnders*?).

There are even madder techniques but I don't want to get prosecuted for manslaughter so I'll let you find out for yourself.

PIPES

If you want to smoke a pipe (no idea what you'd put in it), you wrap up a section of those tin containers, then just fold it slightly at the smoking end so the smouldering whatever isn't flung down your trachea.

KETTLES

Some prisons have an urn from which you have to collect your hot water in a flask before bang up. As everyone always collects their water at the same time and the urn is tiny, only about ten people on the whole wing get hot water. People did some insane moves like connecting a sheathed kettle lead to a metal tray to heat water but I would 100 per cent stay away. Not willing to lose my life for a cuppa!

STICKY TAPE

Tape isn't allowed in jail but you can cut sticky labels off various products the trim them into strips.

TATTOOS

I'm not going to get into the jail tattoo cliché but all I'm going to say is that UK jail tattoos aren't like Russian works of art, they're more like doodles on a Post-it note about MUM or DAD or ONLY GOD CAN JUDGE ME.

Traditional tattoo inks were made from a paste of wood ash and water. The prison adaptation is soot mixed with either shower gel or distilled prison alcohol as it's a disinfectant. Alternatives include ink from photocopiers, burnt polystyrene and ballpoint pen ink – this shit can definitely give you toxic shock, though.

Stick'n'poke tats are simple. You just attach a needle to a pencil using cotton thread. But making a tattoo machine is much harder and involves melted guitar strings, CD player motors, pencil rubbers and toothbrushes. Have a look on YouTube.

By the way, getting tattoos is an offence in prison so if the screws see new ones appearing then you'll get nicked.

CHATHAM POUCH
It's a case of putting your phone in a mini cereal bag, sealing it with a flame, lubricating it with a bit of margarine and ... now you see me, now you don't.

MAKE A COUNTERFEIT TRACKSUIT
Simple, you get a pen and draw whatever logo you want on it. Maybe write AUTHENTIC underneath so people know it's not fake.

MAKING ROPE
Tear off horizontal sections of bed sheet then tie them together. For this reason half the bed sheets you get in jail are frayed on one side and too narrow to tuck in.

MIRROR SKIM TRANSFER

So once you've been banged up if you need something from your next-door neighbour, you're pretty screwed. One way to transfer stuff is to attach a rope to a mirror (in prison, you get small square plastic mirrors with holes in the corner) and spin it out on to the landing – if you get the right angle it will bounce off the opposite skirting-ledge-thingy and skim under your next-door neighbour's door. They then tie whatever it is you require to the string, you reel it back in and there you have it.

THE HORIZONTAL TOILET TRANSFER

Is the aqueous version of the above. If two people in adjacent cells flush ropes at the same time, with a bit of luck, they get tangled in the drainage. You can then pull things back and forth as long as they're waterproof. This is one way to defeat the screws if they're holding you in seg, waiting for you to shit out a phone.

THE VERTICAL TOILET TRANSFER

If multiple cells are above each other and all flush the toilet at the same time, then there should be no system left in the vertical pipe for a while. An upper person can use a weight (a battery) to pass a string down, a lower-down person can use a hook (coathanger, etc.) to pull it in to their cell. Now you're connected. Without the water you can also talk down the hole or play the digeridoo.

STASHING IN THE U-BEND

Make a waterproof bag, get a rope and tie one end to the bag and one end to a fastening device (improvise something from a paperclip or staple). Flush or push the bag over the U-bend and attach the fastening device to a piece of plumbing within arm's reach. Don't flush the toilet while it's up there (I hope that's very obvious). The burglars know this technique so unless it's an aimless spin, this is a lot of hassle for not much.

STICKING STUFF UP
You're not allowed adhesive tack in jail because it could be used to take an impression of a key. Instead, to stick things you can use toothpaste (lasts about two days and soaks through your pictures), coffee-whitener mixed with a dab of water (as strong as Super Glue, also messes up your pictures) or jam sachets (somewhere in-between, and you've, guessed it, also messes up your pictures).

PAPIER MÂCHÉ
Use toothpaste as glue, with flour smuggled from the kitchen and water. Dry your creation on the radiator pipes. I guess you could make whatever you want – bowls, etc. – but I only ever saw this technique used by a couple old Rastas making dice.

LEAVING YOUR DOOR ON LATCH
This is a bit hard to explain. But if you need to go to the shower or to get food, a good technique is to leave your door on latch: twist the handle fully inwards, pull the door to and let the bolt sit on the rim just before it clunks into the hole. That way your door looks as though it's shut, and if someone tries to open it the spring will release and the bolt will lock. Like I said, it's kind of difficult to explain, but it will become apparent when you attempt it.

KEEPING WARM IN THE WINTER
If corrupt screws don't bring in the drugs and phones, they normally get thrown over the fence and then reeled through the windows using afore-mentioned ropes made of bed sheets. Therefore a lot of jail cells don't have windows that can be smashed, they have vents that often don't close or properly open. To close them you have to glue cardboard over them using coffee whitener paste.

PLUG
Some jails have washing machines but in most you have to wash your clothes by hand. I have no idea why but there were never any plugs so you just have to just scrunch some toilet tissue up and stuff it in the hole ...

JAIL VELCRO
Jail Velcro is used for retrieving parcels from areas you can't easily access. Velcro has two sides, doesn't it? the hooky side and the loopy side. The parcel is covered with the hooky bit of a coat hanger. The loopy side is a draw-string bag, swung from the wing. When the two come in contact that's that, you just pull it in. The funny thing is that just outside the Royal Court of Appeal courtroom where I had my case there's a sculpture of a judge made purely from coat hangers – I wonder if those lot are aware of the irony – I doubt it.

RAZOR-BLADE PLUG
If there's no power in your cell, you can access electricity by sticking a razor blade down the tiny slit between the moving part of a light switch and its backing board.

KETTLE-LEAD SATELLITE DISH
I never saw this but my friend who doesn't lie told me that in HMP Isis, a guy worked out how to connect a kettle lead to the back of the TV and they'd pick up different channels depending on where they aimed it.

ANTI-COCKROACH BED MOAT
To prevent cockroaches climbing up your bed legs, you can sit them in cups filled with water.

CUTTING A HOLE IN YOUR MATTRESS
One for the lifers.

OMU AND CLASSIFICATIONS

The OMU (Offender Management Unit) department decides what category of prisoner you are and subsequently what kind of prison you will end up in. Your categorisation gets reviewed once every six months if you're serving fewer than four years and once every year if your sentence is longer. If you feel that you've been wrongly categorised, you can appeal. Get busy with the standard Comp Forms.

The difference between different jails is vast – they range from high-security institutions that look and feel like a barbed-wire swimming pool to low-security prisons from where you can get home leave. There are so many ins and outs and I'm not going to bore you with the small print (go check PSI 8/2013, 9/2015 and 40/2011 – more details are available on the government's website) but here are the basics of categorisation:

CSC means Closed Supervision Centre. The most extreme units in the UK, prisons within a prison. They are designed for people who 'can't be safely managed in the wider prison system'. I have done months and months and months of 23-hour bang-up in a single cell and still can't imagine being in one of these places. There's a rare interview with an ex-CSC prisoner named Kyle Major on CorporateWatch.net if you want to find more.

A-cat prisons hold those considered a serious risk to the public, police and/or state and/or have the means and motivation to stage a concerted escape attempt. If you're considered a high escape risk, they can categorise you as 'A Cat High Risk' or 'A Cat Exceptional Risk'. Expect extreme surveillance for phone calls, visits and letters and 40-foot walls and netting over the exercise area to prevent a helicopter coming to get you.

B-cat prisons also have 40-foot walls, netting over the exercise area and razor wire everywhere, but they're also scattier. B-cat is the default categorisation for a prisoner entering the system, so they are effectively sorting offices. The population changes every day and you'll meet everyone from triple murderers waiting for extradition to people who haven't paid their television licence fee. Expect a lot of people who've committed small crimes, who don't care about the rules, a lot of fights, a lot of chaos – at least you won't die of boredom. They're generally closer to city centres so you'll get more visits. You might wait MONTHS to get re-categorised (I waited eight), which is bad for prisoners who want to progress with their sentence and very bad value for the tax payer, because high-security prisons are far more expensive to operate. The only people who seem to get processed quickly are celebrities and politicians, who go to open prison almost immediately so they don't see the core insanity of it all.

C-cats sound like an improvement but in my experience they have the worst bits of B-cats (the big fences, the drugs, the 23-hour bang up) but without any of the benefits (proximity to family and the action). Less security, fewer staff and they are situated in the middle of nowhere. If you're a drug addict or you want to use your phone all day, this might be to your liking but personally, I found it very, very depressing. The nothingness of prison is what really kills you and in C-cats, *nothing* happens. Most prisoners are serving longer sentences and are on the 'progressive moves system' (see the IEP System section, pages 35–7, for more details) so they are just trying to avoid adjudications, get their D-cat and get the hell out of there. C-cats are like walking a tightrope and the cocktail of boredom, depression and drugs makes good behaviour a very tall order.

D-cats are 'open prisons'. There are still a lot of fences but the security is a lot less tight and in some you get a key to your own cell and can freely associate. This doesn't mean they are good jails though: some are very badly run, far from where our families live, and again there is that toxic mix of drugs, boredom, depression, idiots who fuck around because they have a determined release date and serious prisoners whose freedom depends on good behaviour. The major benefit of open prisons is ROTL: the possibility of being released on temporary licence.

U-cat means unclassified. This is where unconvicted (remanded) prisoners are kept in Northern Ireland.

JULIA ON FEMALE CATEGORISATION

Categorisation in the female estate works differently to the men's. Officially, there are four categorisations:

Category A: for ladies who have already escaped and those who, if they did escape, would be highly dangerous to the public, police and national security.

Restricted Status: for any female whose escape would pose a significant risk to the general public and needs to be held in designated secure accommodation.

Closed Conditions: for ladies who do not necessarily pose the highest risk to the public, but are still considered too much of a risk for open conditions – therefore are behind the gates and cell doors.

Open: this is for ladies who pose little risk to the public and are somewhat 'trusted' in open

prison conditions. You may find open prisoners in with the general population or some prisons are open or have open units within the grounds on the other side of the fence.

A hot topic at the moment is private vs public prisons. Private prisons are generally shinier, newer and some have in-cell phones and so they are popular with prisoners. They also often have very inexperienced staff and the same levels of reoffending, riots, drugs and complete chaos, plus the added risk of the tax payer footing the bill if they fail. Public prisons, on the other hand, are a total mess because the government really doesn't give a shit, doesn't listen to its own independent investigations and makes the role of chief inspector for prisons untenable. Again, this is a case of C.R.A.P. – there are some private prisons so bad they've been repossessed by the government, and there are some government jails that are better than others. Either way, bad public jails justify radically improving public jails, not handing over contracts to private companies.

ROTL (pronounced to rhyme with 'bottle') means Release On Temporary Licence. You know the boiling frog fable? If you put a frog directly into boiling water it will jump out but if you cook it gradually, it will stay put and cook nicely. Well, ROTL is a similar concept: you are gradually exposed to freedom in the hope that you get accustomed to the outside world and stay there. Town visits, aka townies, aka Resettlement Day Release, are the first step. To get a town visit you'll have to submit the correct paperwork, wait and wait while it's processed and then sit in front of a ROTL board, who will ask you questions like why you want leave and what you'd do if this or that stressful situation arises. And then there you are … on the streets of the local town, feeling the temporary freedom, dressed in civilian clothes and riding a local bus rather than a sweatbox. It can be a very trippy experience even if you've only spent a short time inside but for a lifer who hasn't seen the high street in 20 years, to be dropped into a modern town centre full of iPhones and boarded-up shops must be like Stoke-on-Trent meets *Star Trek*.

Prison hooch gives you wings, and I used to daydream about growing a pair and serenely flying off into the distance while the screws shouted, 'GET DOWN AT ONCE, CATTERMOLE!' So when you're out on a town visit, the idea of running away is an obvious temptation, but a very, very stupid one nonetheless: if you did a runner, the police would be straight on your case with Basset Hounds and local radio would be giving hourly updates about how unapproachable you are. Living life on the run is a prison of sorts (trust me, I've done a fair bit of it) and once caught, they give you extra time and stick you in an E-Suit (a green and yellow chequered jumpsuit with HMPRISON written across the back) and strip you off every single evening.

I can see the temptation for people on indefinite sentences which seem to be impossible to get released from, or those facing parole boards that take six months just to provide a signature but, like I said, if the E-Plans go wrong, you just end up back at square one (more like square minus ten).

All of this considered, it's pretty remarkable that only 0.005 per cent of 333,000 ROTLs in 2016 resulted in failure. And it's pretty remarkable that the media blows a gasket when it does happen. Because of this the Ministry of Justice has decreased use of ROTLs by a third over the last four years despite the fact that they are proven to decrease offending rates and are such a valuable part of reintegration for long-term prisoners.

JULIA'S STORY

I got Child Re-Settlement ROTL so I could leave the prison to see my children. Make sure you get your paperwork in order well in advance – my ROTLs were delayed due to administrative delays and errors, it was so frustrating. I did everything possible my end, but due to several basic mistakes and delays, I was kept waiting. It felt very unjust and I was given so much incorrect information. The result was that I was stressed and my children were disappointed week on week, and believe me, the disappointment runs deep.

Even though I felt like exploding at the sheer incompetence, I kept my cool. Biting your lip is a skill you develop, no point blowing or I wouldn't have got my ROTLs at all.

Not everyone is eligible for ROTL, it depends on you mainly and if you behave! I had visits home to my children, which is integral to making those bonds with your children again. Although my days out were amazing, I was so anxious that I wanted to get back within the prison gates – I was always back hours early for fear of being a minute late!

For the last couple of months of my sentence, I worked out of the jail in a charity shop. A taxi used to collect me from the prison gates in the morning and pick me back up in the afternoon. Only the manager knew that I was on day release from the prison, but I chose to disclose it to other volunteers because it was too complicated to lie. It is, however, up to you – do whatever is comfortable to you.

HDC (Home Detention Curfew, or 'tag') is when you get one of those electronic plastic anklets so the system can monitor where you are at all times. HDC is a sentence they might give you instead of sending you to prison and if you're on a determinate sentence of less than four years, you might get early release if you're considered suitable. Don't hold your breath if you're guilty of crimes aggravated by race, religion or sexuality, and you won't get it for terrorism, offences with explosives or serious crimes against the person – although you'll most likely be serving longer than four years for that anyway.

The tags are the property of the private companies that come round to fix them and if you damage them, you'll face a separate charge. You used to be able to heat up the plastic in a hot bath or with hair straighteners, slip it off your foot, then go down the pub, but it's a bit more tricky these days.

PART THREE: WHAT NEXT?

MOVING PRISONS

People often think that you'll spend your entire sentence in a single jail but in practice it's rarely like this.

There are a number of reasons for getting moved around. You can get recategorised. You can get 'ghosted' if you are seen to be a threat to prisoners, staff or the order of the prison – if you are a persistent headache to the system you will Ride the Ghost Train, getting moved from jail to jail incessantly. Or you can get moved for absolutely no reason other than that they are trying to free up space and redistribute prisoners, i.e. you're serving in overcrowded HMP Wandsworth doing just fine, you have a court date at Highbury Magistrates, a court that discharges to HMP Pentonville, so that's where you end up.

Generally, you get minimal or no notice – a slip under the door after everyone's been locked up, announcing that you'll be moved the next morning. It leaves you no opportunity to tell your people on the outside or say a proper goodbye to the people you've spent every day with for however long. You'll regularly hear people shouting down the wing after bang up, like ...

'CARRRRLLLLLL!'

'YEAH???'

'I'm moving tomorrow ... HMP Berwyn.'

' ... Shit ... I heard that place is a DUMP!'
' ... Say no more!'

In male jails, people depend on each other but generally just 'man-up' so missing someone remains an odd and unspoken energy. In female jails, according to Julia Howard, things can be a lot more emotional ...

JULIA ON LEAVING PRISON

The bond between female prisoners is so strong that once you begin to feel settled, it really feels like a prison family. Then someone goes home (or is moved), or is shipped out to another prison. It feels like your world has ended when your routine breaks. You can prepare for people going home, but when someone is shipped out, they are literally told at eight in the morning and have about an hour to pack all their stuff and go to reception, ready for the sweatbox to take them to a new jail.

Ship-outs are common as there are only a few female jails in the country, especially since HMP Holloway closed in 2016. It is common for girls to move hundreds of miles away from where they live. This has an absolutely massive effect on mental health, family ties and ultimately, puts friends and families under pressure. You never know when a ship-out will be so you live on your nerves that it could be you or one of your friends that will go. Just try and be accepting of what happens. You learn that you can't fight everything; riding the system is like being on a roller coaster in pitch-black dark. Accepting that things aren't fair will help you deal with it. Life isn't always fair, but jail is even less fair.

The next morning you'll be carted off in a sweatbox full of prisoners prophesying about what the food and regime will be like in the new jail. When you arrive at the new prison, you'll be treated like a newbie: this is called 'Lay Down Time'.

Proximity to your home is rarely considered – they end up shipping boys from Swansea to Northumberland, women from the Shetland Islands to Yorkshire. I know so many London boys who were shipped up to HMP Wayland, which is in a remote Norfolk village. It's funny when you think about it; they've lived for years in Norfolk but never seen the medieval houses, the coast or any 'Area of Outstanding Natural Beauty' – they've just seen a big old concrete wall. As Julia already said, being moved hundreds of miles away is a nightmare for the prisoners and their family alike.

If you're moved then ask your contacts on the outside to let everyone know your new location. In theory, letters should get forwarded from your old jail but it could take a while.

PREPARING FOR RELEASE

Fingers crossed, you'll have a home to go to – the shortest of sentences can mean you lose your home because you were unable to pay rent, or you got the boot from your council housing. If you are released without accommodation then I'd suggest you contact the usual homelessness charities but they're unable to help everyone – a shocking number of people are sent from jail to sleep in the street.

If you're coming out on HDC (Home Detention Curfew), parole or ROTL (Release on Temporary Licence) you will need to have accommodation secured and probation will have to check it's all suitable – they will need to know whether there's drug or alcohol use, if a family member is in trouble with the police and whether your family know the truth of the crime because a lot of people play it down or keep it totally secret.

Time slows to a grinding halt the closer you come. If your release date isn't determined then it can get delayed over and over again – personally, I got all my stuff packed up and ready to go three separate times before I was finally let out. The weeks between those days were the slowest of my life, but then again, my situation was minor in comparison to people who get knocked back on their parole for years and years.

When your cell-bye-date finally comes, distribute your belongings amongst your friends on the wing and say your goodbyes – it's a bittersweet feeling as your mates congratulate you while you feel bad just leaving them stuck there.

There's a lot of lore about leaving prison – one myth is that anyone who writes graffiti on the walls will be back to clean it. A second myth is that you shouldn't take your prison clothing with you, but I nicked a pair of jeans and I still wear them and I haven't been ... DON'T JINX IT. A third bit of lore is that if you don't eat your breakfast the morning of release then you'll be back to finish it

– more to the point, getting released takes half the day so I'd suggest you eat the porridge just to avoid getting hangry. The fourth and final thing is a tradition: tell your least favourite screw something along the lines of 'I've done my time, you are doing a life sentence'.

You'll stand there at the gatehouse getting your stored property back (if it hasn't been nicked). They might search you, then they will give you your £46 release grant and travel warrant (unless you were on remand, in which case you'll get absolutely nothing), you'll sign a few bits of paperwork, then you'll be on your way.

RETURNING TO THE REAL WORLD

There you are ... Free with inverted commas, Free with a capital F ... It should be the biggest day of your life but in my case I was sat in the drizzle outside the prison gates in a town I'd never heard of with £46 in cash and all my belongings in a big bag plastered with HM PRISON logos.

Like most people, I walked from the gates on my own – unlucky people are met by the police, who are there to 'gate arrest' you for another charge, lucky people are met by loved ones.

A countryside bus came towards me at 25mph and it was the fastest-moving thing I'd seen for a very long time. I hadn't touched cash for months, but now I was under pressure to pay the bus conductor with an audience of grannies looking me up and down. I reached the train station and I swear the train home felt more like a shuttle to the moon than the delayed departure to Essex.

There are some short-term practicalities for you to deal with: you'll have your first non-prison food and then you'll have to go for an introductory appointment with your probation officer at the office nearest your accomodation.

Then it's the start of the head spin: freedom is hard to take at face value once it's been taken away from you, the freedom you knew from before just isn't the same when you return. Slowly, you'll begin to re-learn the matrix of everyday life: for me, it was rediscovering how the rain and the sun felt on my face and I nearly fell through doors because they were so light. I logged on to the internet and it made my brain feel like a cyber anxiety landfill. I got used to having pockets full of things like money and keys, and I slowly learnt that people who were being kind didn't have an ulterior motive. Those were the noticeable things. The major aspects of reintegration are often much harder to identify because no one explains explicitly what you've had taken away – privacy, dignity, trust, choice, being your true self.

I got along alright with my probation officer, though – I always felt like they would've helped me more if they had the resources. As it was, they just needed to tick boxes and achieve targets. They basically sat there repeating that song from *Trainspotting*, telling me to 'choose life, choose a job, choose a career, choose a family', all while I was sat there thinking, 'I can barely choose a flavour of pot noodle in the Co-op.'

Jail takes your responsibilities (or lack of them) away from you and I guess that's what people who have issues with addiction or who have grown up without family subconsciously find reassuring about the jail environment. Rules are the opposite of choices, choice underpins every element of the free world so when you are thrown back, at a time when making the right choices is more crucial than ever, you are at your least practised.

Institutionalisation is a massive word. It's eight syllables long and I misspell it every time, but I could write 1,000 pages about its meaning. In prison they never even tell you about it, but it's a phenomenon that anyone who has been through the system will fully connect with once they understand: prison creates massive voids in your head and the institution fills them in. Prison lives in me, in the way I avoid eye contact with people I just met, the way I recklessly ride a motorbike, shrink into myself, feel irrationally aggressive, feel much more able to break the law because I don't give a shit if I go back to prison ... It's all of those things and a million more. If you've been through it then you'll be able to list off your own personal million.

Traumatic experiences in early life throw spanners into your development: they freeze you into childish behaviours, sometimes including criminality, and then jail drops the temperature even further. I know a lot of notoriously hard geezers and supposedly scary gangsters these days, but all I can see is vulnerability – violent and vulnerable is a very common combination. Acting bad doesn't come from their soul, it's just a form of compensation, and the more vulnerable they are, the harder they act just to cover it all up. But the point is, loads of people characterised as the enemy by mainstream society are fully rescuable.

A majority of ex-prisoners commit crime after release – a massive 61 per cent of people get arrested. This proportion drops to just 19 per cent when people are in employment – it's obvious why, isn't it? More community involvement, more trust, more financial security. After prison I borrowed money, stole my lunch, worked warehouse jobs, cash-in-hand industrial jobs with chemicals that nuked my brain, then got more stable carpentry jobs through friends that didn't require formal job applications. Applying for a more legitimate job is a different story – you'll probably have to tick a box saying you have a criminal record and most likely, being honest will result in your application getting fast-forwarded to the bin. Applications should be a lot more nuanced: only when a crime is relevant to the job should it warrant attention. When an irrelevant conviction you already served the punishment for ends up overshadowing the rest of your working life it's so deeply unfair, but that's where we're at.

I would love to walk into an interview saying 'I committed x-crime for x-reason and this job would really help me get back on my feet so maybe I'd be the best employee you've ever had' or 'I was excellent at selling drugs so maybe my skills could be transferred and I'd be able to sell double glazing for you'. But while the system is as it is, personally I'd lie on the application and hope they didn't find out. As I said right at the beginning of the book, being honest with dishonest systems is a waste of time.

If you get to the interview stage and prison is out in the open for discussion, then inside responsibilities (Insider, Listener, Toe By Toe mentor, etc.) can potentially help you as they show that you did something positive with your time.

Employers who have recruited ex-prisoners have often found that they value the job more than most as they're eager not to go back to prison. Timpson has led the way and deserve a special shout-out – 10 per cent of the high street key cutters' employees are ex-prisoners. One of my mates got on this scheme and absolutely loves it.

Looking now, there are a bunch of charities that can help you while you're on the wing, but besides St Giles Trust when I needed them the most, I wasn't even aware of them, let alone receiving an info pack or an appointment. If you're currently serving, it's definitely worth being pro-active and looking these things up.

I should say that for every negative judgement from someone with power, there are hundreds of possible connections with good people – I've actually ended up on jobs where half the team has been in prison at some point and this offers connections and besides job stuff, I've met librarians with the dots on their knuckles (ACAB anti-police tattoos), bus drivers with swallows on their hands and seemingly straight-and-narrow journalists who have come to interview me and told me once upon a time, they did a stint in borstal. For me, it's really helped being unashamed about my past but I'm probably an anomaly – for the average person it's prudent to keep that whole part of your life a secret.

After I'd been released people would ask me about the BLOOD and the GUTS and the VIOLENCE. Someone even asked me, 'So, did you have to join the Bloods or the

Crips or the Aryan Brotherhood?' I responded that 'Mum wouldn't be best pleased if I shaved off my eyebrows and replaced them with tribal tattoos.' I wish more people had asked me searching questions. It's tricky. The very subtle things that jail takes from you are hard to ask about, but if someone asks questions that add texture to the experience then maybe they'll get to those more subtle core issues. But, yeah, British people and their emotions, especially those who've just come from an environment where you wear a mask 24/7 – encouraging a prisoner to talk can be like trying to get a cat out from under the sofa when it knows you are taking it to the vet: if you get too close, it'll disappear out the cat flap.

I was lucky enough to end up in a relationship with a girl who asked great questions and if I hadn't, then maybe I wouldn't be able to discuss this jail stuff as I do. I already told you, but I should tell you another million times – emotional support is such a massive privilege. So many prisoners are released to no home, no support and no love. That £46 release grant can buy a couple of bottles of whisky or a couple bags of heroin and to state the obvious, they aren't long-term solutions but quick fixes are often all that is on offer for some people in the current political climate. On that note: if you commute between your stable job and your stable house and intersect a homeless guy with neither of those then just give them some money and don't patronise them about what they decide to do with it.

It's difficult when you feel that the world, including your family, has moved on without you and while you might make a resolution to 'be a good person/mother/father/ partner', the reality can be a lot more challenging. While you're behind bars relationships can change dramatically – strong blokey blokes can become emotionally needy, really positive people can start to feel really down – support should be unconditional and long term, so remember the positive aspect of the person before they went in and if you can wait for that person to come back around then you should. Everyone involved can have unrealistic expectations of one another. It's extremely difficult trying to be a person that you might never have been before.

Another bunch with unrealistic expectations are probation officers and certain other official bodies who always focus on those who went clean and stayed out of prison and really turned their life into something – they will probably tell you about this twat called Carl, who wrote a book. I apologise in advance. The whole idea of 'Going Straight' often sets you up to fail – no one is 'straight' – from myself who reoffended the day I walked out the gates but never got arrested all the way to the career politicians who created this toxic environment but haven't broken a law.

I see my friends trying to pull it off. They used to wear head-to-toe fluffy white Kangol tracksuits in their drug dealing days and now they've been released from prison and they can't get employed and are in the dole office getting their benefits cut off for no apparent reason, and they've got to go to WHSmith to steal a Mars Bar and go back to a house with no heating. What do you do? Do you A) go through the massive slog to get the sanctions on your benefits lifted? Or

B) go and see your mate who can hook you up with a bit of gear and you can make a grand in half an hour?

I'm not suggesting you should relapse, reoffend and re-enter jail ... I'm just saying we need to be realistic about a rigged system.

Anyway, I'm getting carried away. Back to the longer-term practicalities. 'Licence' is the period after your custodial sentence – you're still serving but they allow you to live in the community. However, if you stray too far or mis-behave then you'll get yanked by the neck and recalled back into prison. You will have what are called Licence Conditions – at the very least you'll have to attend pro-bation appointments, inform them of your whereabouts, stay at a designated address and not go abroad.

Recall is as it sounds – it means getting sent back to jail. For people serving fixed-term sentences there is initially a 28-day recall (or 14 if your sentence is less than a year). A standard recall is where you spend the entirety of your licence in prison. L-platers (lifers) and the extended sen-tence crew can apply to have their licence revoked after a decade of good behaviour but you'll have a drama getting out – it can take years literally and this includes if you were recalled for an unfounded allegation. You can appeal most of these decisions – ask PAS or *Inside Time* or a solicitor for all the fiddly bits.

Probation needs its own book. In recent years, due to bungled privatisation it has changed so much that even probation staff don't seem to understand the set-up. The NPS (National Probation Service) manage 'higher-risk' individuals. Private CRCs (Community Rehabilitation Companies) manage 'lower-and medium-risk offenders' and are paid according to their results. Your appoint-ments will go from weekly to monthly and then perhaps even less regular, until the point you get off licence.

In the much longer term the effect of prison on a lot of peo-ple, including myself, is that if I'm feeling crap about my life,

I will often feel like returning to a cell. The outside world is free but unpredictable. Jail is shit, but at least it's comprehensible: it offers a filtered humanity you can format yourself against. For those of an institutionalised or feral disposition, the potential violence of fights in jail is preferable to the real world violence of a letterbox full of bills and bailiff letters. Prison is a pre-modern world, a cell is literally like a cave, the days have definite cycles and there's no Wi-Fi interfering with your attention span.

The PTSD is real and it stays with you, it gets triggered easily. I swear half of drill music by the roguest of kids is about this stuff. For me it's funny, that T2 song 'Heartbroken' was played all the time on my wing so now when it gets played at a party, everyone else is loving it, and singing along while I'm on some Vietnam shit, looking at my pint and thinking … fucking hell!

PROACTIVE ACTION

The first suggestion is small, but it all starts with words we use. Think about it. Who did the 'offenders' offend? Why are children who've committed a crime suddenly called 'youths'? Why talk about 'rehabilitation' like it's the answer when if people weren't debilitated, they wouldn't need to be rehabilitated? What is a 'reform' if it really means building a USA-style private 'super prison' over the hills and far away?

Maybe you should buy your MP a copy of this book. The prison system is inhumane, illogical, really expensive and it creates more crime than it stops. A justice secretary with real vision and resources could go down in history, but as it currently stands, being the Justice Secretary is the shortest of straws when it comes to political positions. Over the last decade justice secretaries and prison ministers have served shorter sentences than most prisoners, and that's really saying something.

The funny (not funny) thing is that the Ministry of Justice acts a lot like friends I've had who are at the pits of their drug addiction. I don't mean to insult drug users by comparing the two, but they are alike in some way: they often break promises, miss deadlines and try to cover it all up so they can continue as per usual with their habit. Some people say that drug users need to hit 'rock bottom' before they confront their problems and it seems the justice system is now at that point – it needs to tackle the core reasons beyond the headlines of self-harm, suicides and reoffending rates, and enact a much wider radical change.

But, the thing is, the MoJ is under the control of its pimp: the media. Fear and sensation sells newspapers, it's a pantomime, and we – the criminals – are the bad guys. Only around 70 prisoners are serving full life sentences, but we're all characterised as psychos and paedophiles. Just imagine the beatdown the media would give the government if they reduced prisoner numbers or if they increased spending on prisons, or even if they gave prisoners healthy food – the 'LAGS GET SALAD' headline could literally end a minister's career, so I doubt they'll give us edible food any time soon.

Is the system totally broken, or is this how it's intended to be? If you were to build a justice system from scratch, you'd be a very twisted psychopath to build it this way. Which makes me ask – do me and you have the same lightbulb above our heads? Is it less about little tweaks, more about a complete overhaul? Any positive change would be welcome at this point, but it's not about returning the shit standards of pre-austerity 2010 jail, it's not about stopping at a 'Scandinavian model', it's about questioning the very recent invention of this whole concept of prisons that has somehow become the status quo.

Some of the work that legitimate charities do behind the scenes is incredible – fighting cases for people who can't get legal aid, lobbying and providing jobs for ex-offenders. What I'm saying though is that all big movements towards social justice – workers' rights, women's rights, race rights, gay rights – have required radical direct action. Prison simply hasn't yet had that. This issue is next on society's to-do list so don't roll over, no more dead-scrolling on social media, get active.

If you are an ex-prisoner or someone you know is serving and you have the capacity then start your own campaign group. Join CAPE – they organise direct action protests against the massive new wave of prison expansion. Get involved or get guidance from them. Look up your local anarchist groups – forget what you've heard, anarchists have done valuable prisoner support work for years for purely altruistic reasons. Maybe you're a creative person who can contribute video editing, copywriting or photography (there are plenty of organisations in need of these skills) – send me an email. Or maybe you currently give a standing order to a crap overfunded charity who spend it on central London offices – cancel it and send me an email. I'll tell you who really needs your money. Maybe you're a rich person who can give an amount that will totally revolutionise the capabilities of a group who have all the time and guts but don't even have enough to take the train to the sites where these new superprisons are being built? If you're legally trained then Howard League for Penal Reform and The Prison Reform Trust do great things. Become a McKenzie Friend, have a look at their website to learn more. And make sure you listen to Novara's 'The Lockdown' podcast, which gives excellent insight into criminal justice issues.

Or get us, ex-prisoners, to come and talk in your local area – there are so many great ex-prisoners in this country who can definitely keep an audience entertained for two hours straight. Basically, if you want to help, then connecting with prisons and prisoners is the first step. You should do all the little things you can, like visiting your local prison and walking around the perimeter.

Most importantly, don't forget your people on the wing – it's easy to do because it's so hectic once you return to the outside world but make a conscious effort to keep in touch with prisoners inside. Set alarms on your phone to remind you to send them books and CDs, and visit, if possible. If you're going to commit a crime, utilise your newfound criminal mastery and the connections that you learnt in jail and don't get caught. And if you're inside right now, then BANG THAT DOOR!

PART FOUR: RESOURCES

THINGS TO TAKE WITH YOU

As I mentioned earlier, when you go to court, you should take a 'bang up bag' of essentials with you. I did already say that some prisons have their 'Facilities List' available online – but if not, then this is a rough guide to what I'd recommend taking with you:

A list of contacts – phone numbers, birth dates and addresses. **Cash** – for canteen. Take whatever you might have spare. **Sliders or flip flops** – when you see the state of the prison showers – cockroaches and slime on the floor – you'll thank me for this suggestion. **Stereo** – totally invaluable (the requirements might be on the jail's facility list – most B–cats don't allow detachable speakers, a model like Panasonic RX–ES27 is perfect). **CDs and tapes** – 30 maximum and no copies (although I had about 60 and they were all copied). **Over-ear headphones** – the closest you'll get to privacy, they can't be wireless. **Foam earplugs** – in case you pelly up with a chainsaw snorer. **Comfy shoes** – they won't find you not-guilty because you're wearing Prada loafers, so pack something practical. **Smelly shoes** – for the gym. **Photos of loved ones** – that's obvious. **Stamps and envelopes. Stationery** – just a couple pencils and pens – it really hits home that you're not at home

when you can't find a decent ballpoint pen for weeks on end. **Alarm clock** – but you'll wake up regardless when that door clunks. **Basic toiletries** – toenail clippers, a toothbrush, etc. **Books** – I doubt they'll let you have them, but worth a try. **Towel** – prison towels are disgusting. **Bed sheets/pillow covers** – ditto. **Clothes** – male prisoners won't be allowed their own unless on remand or Enhanced IEP. You're not allowed anything that could hide your identity (no hoodies, no balaclavas, no ski-masks), or be used to impersonate a staff member (no dark blue or black items), start arguments (no sports teams or national team jerseys although my mate wore his head-to-toe Albania trackie 365 days a year), or used as a weapon (sovereign rings or stilettos). **A comfy trackie** is a must. **Shorts** for the gym.

PRISON LEXICON

Prison slang changes from region to region, it's a mix everything that's in the area: cockney rhyming, Yardy patois, Romany Cant, Gaelic, bits of Bengali. It changes every day ... a bitty becomes a nitty becomes a kitty ... and if you use the version from a few weeks ago then the kids will look at you like you're from the Stone Age.

A four, a two, a nine, etc. – a four/two/nine-year sentence etc., i.e. I got a four, not bad, was expecting a ten. **A four stretch, two stretch, nine stretch, etc.** – the same, doing a stretch is doing a sentence. **The ones/twos/threes/fours** – the floor of the wing; 'I'm on the ones', etc. **ACAB** – All Cops are Bastards, a seventies acronym widely used by punks and criminals (my school bus driver had it on his knuckles) (also, **1312** means the same thing – first letter, third letter, etc.) (also, **HWDP** is the same in Polish, it's widely seen in UK prisons). **Acki** (also, **Ak**) – a fellow Muslim. **Bang the Door** – prison tradition of making a racket by booting your cell door, particularly on New Year's Eve or when someone's escaped on *Crimewatch*. **Bang up** – period of time when your door is locked, can also mean to beat someone up. **Bang weights** – do weights. **Bare** – a lot (was Jamaican, but now common). **Baron** – prison money lender. **Barry** – cocaine. **Bash** – wank. **Basic-rider** – someone who loves riding basic regime. **Beg/beg–it/beg-friend** – sycophant. **Bent-up** – to be overzealously restrained by screws. **Bilk** – to do a runner without paying. **Bin** – prison 'man's in bin'. **Bird** – a prison sentence, i.e. 'Carl is doing bird'. **Bitty/nitty/kitty/baghead** – an addict or generally rattling person. **Blag/blagger** – old-school cockney for armed robbery/robber. **Block** – solitary confinement. **Blue box** – payphone. **Bobby** – heroin. **Boogooyaga** – Jamaican word for a degenerate. **Borstal** – young offenders' institution (comes from the Kent village where the original prison for children was). **Budgies** – body – obsessed prisoners who spend half their time in the gym, the other half looking in the mirror. **Bups** – to rip someone off. **Burglars** – Dedicated Search Team (DST) screws. **Burn/Snout** – tobacco. **C.R.A.P.** – Confusing Rules Applied Patchily. **Carpet** – Three-month sentence. (Three-months was the time it took to make a rug for a cell). **CHIMPS** – Police Community Support Officers, officers who support the police community, Completely Hopeless In Most Policing Situations, Snitches with Badges. **China** – mate (cockney) (mate>china plate>china). **Chip** – to leave (cockney). **Chip net** – the suicide prevention net strung between landings (it prevents you from chipping). **Danny** – foil (for smoking heroin): Danny Boyle>foil. **Diesel** – tea. **Dipping** – stealing. **Dog ends** – cigarette butts. **Double Bubble** – to pay back double what you borrowed (shit APR). **Eci** – old cockney slang for police, comes from if you look in the rear-view mirror at police it says 'ecilop'. **E–Suit/Clown Suit/Banana Suit** – green and yellow suits worn by **E–Men** who've attempted to do the **E–Word** or are on the **E–List**. **Enhanced** – Those with greater privileges. **Firm** – a gang. **Fraggle** – a weak–minded person. **Fraggle Rock** – psychiatric unit. **Free Flow (aka Moves)** – The ten-minute period where you can transfer between different areas of prison. **Ghost** – to get moved from a prison with no notice whatsoever to maintain order. **Riding The Ghost Train** means to do your whole sentence getting ghosted from place to place. **Going Over** – overdosing. **Grass** – a snitch. **Green/Lean/Dank/Lemon/Haze/Cro** – million words for weed, but I don't smoke that shit so don't ask me. **Guv** – a prison officer. **Hench** – muscular person, a beefcake. **Jack the Rippers** – rhyming slang for prison slippers. **Jam roll** – rhyming slang for parole but also a Polish person. **Joey** – 1) a plugged or swallowed drugs parcel (from the way a kangaroo carries its young), 2, a subservient prisoner who does another's dirty work. **Jug** – to throw hot water (often mixed with sugar) in someone's face. **Kanga, Scooby Dr Who The Who** – old-school bits of rhyming slang for prison officer screw. **Keep dog** – to watch out for someone; keep dog for me (spy>doggy's eye>dog).

Kick – sludgy sediment for making hooch. **Knock Back** – an official refusal: 'I got knocked back by the parole board'. **Lag** – tabloid word for any prisoner but by the book it means someone serving over two years. **Lagboat/Lagging** – drunk. **L-plates** – life sentence. **Lump** – a long sentence. **Mattress Job** – where the police or prison officers cover you with a mattress before beating you; causes internal bruising so you have no visible evidence of being brutalised (Brixton and Stoke Newington police station 1980s racist speciality but still in use). **Mazza** – a madness, a drama; hype, either good or bad. **Meds** – medicine or the medical hatch. **Moon** – old slang for month; prisoners didn't have calendars or clocks so would watch the sun and moon instead. **Mug Off** – to disrespect someone. **NASA** – nice and safe armpits. **Nonce/Bacon/Animal** – so many bits of slang for a sex offender (people are obsessed); nonce comes from HMP Wakefield, where sex offenders were deemed Not On Normal Courtyard Exercise to keep them protected. **Nosh/ Noddy/Uckaz/Brain** – blowjob (again, more slang than I can list). **Numbers/Cucumbers** – VPU (Vulnerable Persons Unit) where at-risk prisoners are held (sex offenders, debtors, grasses). **On Top** – authorities giving you attention, i.e. "That was a bit on top". **Pelly/Pad/Peter** – cell, to pelly/pad/peter up is to share a cell; a pelly/pad/peter thief is the lowest of the low, who will traditionally get a cell door slammed on their fingers. **Phone Line** – a scar from mouth to ear, usually done to show the man is a police informant. **Plug** – to hide something in your Chatham Pouch. **Pony** – crap, in both senses. **Prop** – your stored property. **Quack** – prison doctor (the story of this slang is very interesting, but too long for now). **Radio Rental/Chicken Oriental** – issues of the mental kind. **Riding** – to spend time in prison 'riding bang up'. **Rub Down** – a cell search. **Ain't got a Scooby** – I don't know; I mean I *do* know, it means I don't know. **Screw Boy** – someone who wants to be friends with the officers. **Send-out** – someone who is made to do things by other prisoners. **Shank/Chef/Skeng/Tool/April/Shiv** – a knife (first three are newer road slang, last three are old school). **Shipped Out** – to be moved from one prison to another. **Shit and a shave** – a brief sentence because you only have time to do the above before release. **Shit Up** – when a screw has a bucket of shit thrown over them. **SN** – say *nothinggg* – means nothing but certain people say this non-stop, even before anything's been said. **Snout** – a cigarette or tobacco. **SO** – senior officer. **Sock Rock** – improvised weapon made from a pool ball in a sock. **Sosh** – association/social time. **Spin** – a cell search. **Starred Up** – getting transferred from children's prison to adult prison at a younger age than required. **Straightener** – organised fight to straighten things out. **Strap/Growler/Bucky/Piece/Leng/Shooter** – there are a million bits of slang for gun – **nostrils** is a sawn-off. **Sweatbox** – prison van. **Tear Up** – a fight. **Tech/Blower/Zanco** – mobile phone. **The Out/road** – the outside world: 'I'll do this and that when I'm on the out', 'I'm soon on road'. **Tick** – to borrow drugs or tobacco. **Track Marks** – scars from injecting heroin. **Tram Lines/Mars Bar** – the scar left by two razors separated by a millimetre or two apart cannot be stitched and looks like a mess. **Undies** – standard British slang for underwear; also means undercover police. **Window Warrior** – someone who anonymously shouts insults out the windows after the cell doors are shut. **Wire** – improvised charging cable for your phone. **Womble** – litte picker. **Wonga** – money. **Wrap Up/Twist up** – to beat someone, normally by authorities. **Yute** – a boy. **Ting** – literally any of the above.

And here are commonly used bits of official jargon:

ACCT – Assessment Case in Custody and Teamwork. **A-Cat** – maximum security prison. **Adjudication** – where you appear before a governor for some wrongdoing. **B-CAT** – medium – security prison. **CALM** – Controlling Anger and Learning to Manage It. **C-Cat** – medium security prison. **CRAMS** – Case Recording and Management System. **CRB** – Criminal Records Bureau. **CRC** – Community Rehabilitation Company. **CRD** – Conditional Release

Date. **D-Cat** – an open prison. **DIP** – Drug Intervention Programme. **DIRF** – Discrimination Incident Report Form. **DJ** – District Judge. **DPP** – Detention for Public Protection (indefinite sentence for children). **DRR** – Drug Rehabilitation Requirement. **DST** – Dedicated Search Teams. **DTTO** – Drug Treatment and Testing Order. **DTU** – Drug Testing Unit. **EPP** – Extended Public Protection Sentence (the new name for IPP, don't know why they bothered). **ETS** – Enhanced Thinking Skills. **HDC** – Home Detention Curfew. **HMCTS** – Her Majesty's Court and Tribunal Service. **HMIP** – Her Majesty's Inspector of Probation. **HMP** – Her Majesty's Prison. **HMPPS** – Her Majesty's Prison and Probation Service. **Hooch** – homebrewed alcohol. **IDTS** – Integrated Drug Treatment System. **IEP** – Incentive Earned Privileges. **IMB** – Independent Monitoring Board. **Insider** – accredited prisoner who provides advice to others. **IPCC** – Independent Police Complaints Commission (notoriously un-independent). **ISP** – Indeterminate Sentence Prisoners, the umbrella term for life, IPP and DPP sentences. **IP** – Properly in Possession. **IPP** – Indeterminate Public Protection Sentence. **JR** – Judge's Remand. **LDU** – Local Delivery Unit. **Listener** – a Samaritans accredited prisoner who supports others. **Lockdown** – to cancel all normal activities and keep prisoners locked up. **MAPPA** – Multi Agency Public Protection Arrangements, the process through which police/probation/prison synergise to manage the risks posed by violent and sexual offenders living in the community. **MDT** – Mandatory Drug Testing. **MoJ** – Ministry of Justice. **NACRO** – National Association for the Care and Resettlement of Offenders. **NAPO** – National Association of Probation Officers. **NOMS** – National Offender Management System. **NPR** – National Prison Radio. **NPS** – National Probation Service. **NTRG** – National Technical Response Group. **OASys** – Offender Assessment System. **OBPS** – Offender Behaviour Programmes. **OM** – Offender Manager. **OMU** – Offender Management Unit. **PAS** – Prisoner Advice Service. **PO** – prison officer. **PPO** – Prolific and Priority Offenders. **PSO/**

PSI – prison service orders, which are gradually being replaced by prison service instructions. **PSR** – Pre-Sentence Report. **Remand** – when you are awaiting sentencing or charge and have been denied bail. **ROCB** – Remanded on Conditional Bail. **ROTL** – Release On Temporary Licence. **SCT** – Safer Custody Team. **Seg** – segregation unit. **SOPO** – Sex Offending Prohibition Order. **SOTP** – Sex Offender Treatment Programme. **SCT** – Secure Training Centre. **TM** – Team Manager. **TWOC** – Take Without Owner's Consent (also a verb … I TWOCed it). **VDT** – voluntary drug testing. **VO** – Visiting Order. **VPU** – Vulnerable Prisoners Unit. **YOI** – Young Offender Institution (jail for kids).

USEFUL CONTACTS

Practical support for current prisoners

Bent Bars Project
A penpal project which provides additional support to LGBTQI prisoners in Britain.
PO Box 66754, London WC1A 9BF
bent.bars.project@gmail.com
www.bentbarsproject.org

Cruse Bereavement
Supporting the recently bereaved.
Unit 1, 1 Victoria Villas, Richmond,
TW9 2GW
0844 477 9400
www.cruse.org.uk

Haven Distribution
A charity that provides books for prisoners.
27 Old Gloucester Street, London WC1N 3XX
www.havendistribution.org.uk/

Inside Time
A newspaper for prisoners, available in the prison libraries and in visitors' centres.
https://insidetime.org/

Koestler Trust
Helping prisoners to lead more positive lives by encouraging them to make art and music.
168a Du Cane Road, London W12 OTX
www.koestlertrust.org.uk/about-us

Prison Choir Project
Reducing reoffending, building self-esteem, improving self-confidence and employability – through collaborative music-making.
www.prisonchoirproject.co.uk

Prisoners' Advice Service
Offering free legal advice to all prisoners.
PO BOX 46199, London EC1M 4XA
020 7253 3323
www.prisonersadvice.org.uk

Prisoners' Education Trust
Since 1989, the Prisoners' Education Trust has been providing access to broader learning opportunities for prisoners to enhance their chances of building a better life after release. www.prisonerseducation.org.uk/

Prisons and Probation Ombudsman
Carries out independent investigations into deaths and complaints in custody.
Ashley House, 2 Monck Street, London SW1P 2BQ
www.ppo.gov.uk

Samaritans
Providing emotional support for those struggling.
Freepost RSRB-KKBY-CYJK, PO BOX 9090, Stirling, FK8 2S

116 123 (free day or night)
www.samaritans.org

Shannon Trust
An excellent charity that helps the massive number of
illiterate prisoners to read and write.
89 Albert Embankment, London SE1 7TP
www.shannontrust.org.uk/

The Forward Trust (formerly RAPt, Rehabilitation for Addicted Prisoners Trust)
Aids people with drug and alcohol dependency in
order to help both afflicted individuals and society.
The Foundry, 2nd Floor, 17 Oval Way, London SE11 5RR
020 3752 5560
www.forwardtrust.org.uk/

The Home Office
The official government website for the Home Office.
2 Marsham Street, London SW1P 4DF
020 7035 4848
www.gov.uk/government/organisations/home-office

The Irene Taylor Trust
Using music to support NEET (Not in Employment,
Education or Training) young people, ex-prisoners and
people of all ages in prisons.
7–14 Great Dover Street, London SE1 4YR
www.irenetaylortrust.com

Vegan Prisoner Support Group
Supporting vegans in prison.
BM 2107, London WC1N 3XX
info@vpsg.org
www.vpsg.org/

Women in Prison
Supporting female prisoners.

2nd Floor, Elmfield House, 5 Stockwell Mews, London
SW9 9GX
www.womeninprison.org.uk

Support for families

Action for Prisoners' and Offenders' Families
Works for the benefit of prisoners' and offenders'
families by supporting families who are affected by
imprisonment.
49–51 East Road, London N1 6AH
www.familylives.org.uk/about/our-services/
action-for-prisoners-and-offenders-families

Assisted Prison Visits
Official government guidance for those seeking
financial assistance for prison visits.
assisted.prison.visits@noms.gsi.gov.uk
0300 063 2100
www.gov.uk/help-with-prison-visits

Birth Companions
Supporting pregnant women and mothers behind bars.
Dalton House, 60 Windsor Avenue, London SW19 2RR
www.birthcompanions.org.uk

Families Outside
Supporting families in Scotland affected by
imprisonment.
www.familiesoutside.org.uk

Partners of Prisoners
Providing support services at all stages of the
criminal justice system, from the arrest of a loved one
through to the first steps towards resettlement.
1079 Rochdale Road, Manchester M9 8AJ
mail@partnersofprisoners.co.uk
www.partnersofprisoners.co.uk/

Prisoners' Families Helpline
Provides advice and information on all aspects from
what happens on arrest, visiting a prison to preparing
for release. For prisoners in England and Wales.
0808 808 2003
www.prisonersfamilies.org/

www.prisonbag.com
An excellent blog by a woman whose husband is
serving time for fraud.

www.prisonchatuk.com
An online community for those with a loved one inside
the British prison system.

www.prisonersfamiliesvoices.blogspot.com
A blog written by the families of prisoners.

Ongoing support for life after prison

Unlock
Provides information, advice, training and advocacy
to those dealing with the ongoing effects of criminal
convictions, particularly in relation to jobs.
01634 247350
advice@unlock.org.uk
www.unlock.org.uk

www.prisonerben.blogspot.co.uk
A blog by an ex-prisoner that's funny and on-point.

Prison campaign groups and researchers

Anarchist federations are full of good people who
want to help prisoners (and burn down the prison
system). They often list prisoners' addresses if you'd
like to write to someone.

Empty Cages Collective
Fight for prison abolition and against prison
expansion, building a movement to dismantle the
prison industrial complex in England, Wales and
Scotland.
info@prisonabolition.org

Anarchist Black Cross local branches:

ABC
Brighton
PO Box 74, Brighton BN1 4ZQ
brightonabc@riseup.net

ABC
Bristol
Kebele, 14 Robertson Road,
Easton, Bristol BS5 6JY
www.bristolabc.wordpress.com
bristol_abc@riseup.net

ABC
Cardiff
Red & Black Umbrella, 57–58 Clifton Street, Cardiff
CF24 1LS
www.abccardiff.wordpress.com
cardiff_abc@riseup.net

ABC
Leeds
145–149 Cardigan Road, Leeds LS6 1LJ
www.leedsabc.org
leedsabc@riseup.net

ABC
London
www.network23.org/londonabc/
london_abc@riseup.net

Community Action on Prison Expansion
A grassroots coaliction of local groups organising
against prison expansion in England, Wales and
Scotland.
www.cape.campaign.org

Critical Resistance
Seeks to build an international movement to end the
prison industrial complex.
www.criticalresistance.org

Howard League for Penal Reform
Campaigning for prison reform and making the case
for putting fewer people in prison.
1 Ardleigh Road, London N1 4HS
0207 249 7373
www.howardleague.org/

Incarcerated Workers Organising Committee
The UK branch of International Workers of the Ward,
who organise various prisoner solidarity and prison
labour campaigns
www.iwoc.iww.org.uk

Make Justice Work
A campaign to highlight the wastefulness of short-
term prison sentences and promote
community sentences.
020 3538 8365
www.makejusticework.org.uk

Miscarriages of Justice UK
Campaigning to address miscarriages of justice in the
prison system.
www.majuk.org.uk.

NACRO
A social justice charity with the aim of reducing
crime and assisting resettlement in the sensible

way, through housing support, education provision, addiction support and lobbying the government.
020 7840 6464
https://www.nacro.org.uk/

Prison Reform Trust
The Prison Reform Trust write really clear documents about various issues in the prison system. You don't have to be a criminology graduate to get into them.
15 Northburgh Street, London EC1V 0JR
0808 802 0060
www.prisonreformtrust.org.uk/ForPrisonersFamilies/Whocanhelp

Racial Justice Network
Addressing racial injustice and the legacies of colonialism.
www.racialjusticenetwork.co.uk.

Reclaim Justice Network
Works to radically reduce the size and scope of criminal justice systems and build effective and fair alternatives.
www.reclaimjusticenetwork.org.uk

Smash IPP
An organisation working with IPP prisoners and their Families.
www.smashipp.noflag.org.uk

The Audre Lorde Project's Safe OUTside the System Collective
Organising efforts for safe community resistance of police violence.
www.alp.org/programs/sos

www.solitaryconfinement.org
The definitive resource for the study of solitary confinement, run by Sharon Shalev.